MW01027763

THE DETR
OF 1967

Great Lakes Books
A complete listing of the books in this series can be found online at
wsupress.wayne.edu

THE DETROIT RIOT
OF 1967

Hubert G. Locke

WAYNE STATE UNIVERSITY PRESS
DETROIT

ISBN 978-0-8143-4377-7 (paper)
ISBN 978-0-8143-4378-4 (e-book)
Library of Congress Control Number: 76079479

Wayne State University Press
Leonard N. Simons Building
4809 Woodward Avenue
Detroit, Michigan 48201-1309

Visit us online at wsupress.wayne.edu

MIDSUMMER MADNESS

How soon from highways and alleys
A raging rabble sallies!
Man, woman, youth, and child
Blindly fall to as if gone wild;
>*And ere the craze lose power*
>*The cudgel blows must shower;*
>*They seek with fuss and pother*
>*The fires of wrath to smother.*
>*God knows how this befell!*
>*'T was like some impish spell!*
Some glowworm could not find his mate;
'T was he aroused this wrath and hate.
The elder's charm—Midsummer eve:
But now has dawned Midsummer day.

RICHARD WAGNER
The Master-Singers of Nuremberg
Act 3, Scene 3

CONTENTS

Contents

II. AN INTERPRETATION OF THE EVENT

Contents

Note of Acknowledgment
All illustrations and map information courtesy
Detroit Police Department, base maps courtesy
Detroit Department Report and Information.

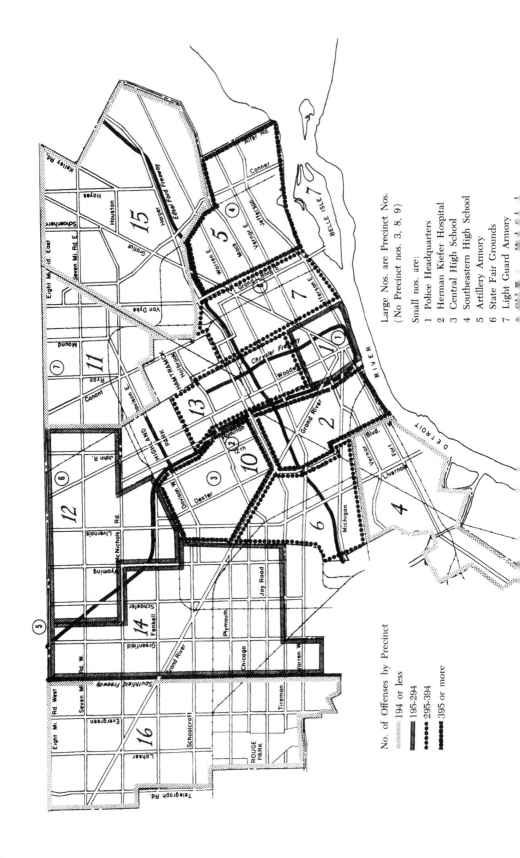

Large Nos. are Precinct Nos.
(No Precinct nos. 3, 8, 9)

Small nos. are:

1 Police Headquarters
2 Herman Kiefer Hospital
3 Central High School
4 Southeastern High School
5 Artillery Armory
6 State Fair Grounds
7 Light Guard Armory

No. of Offenses by Precinct

194 or less
195-294
295-394
395 or more

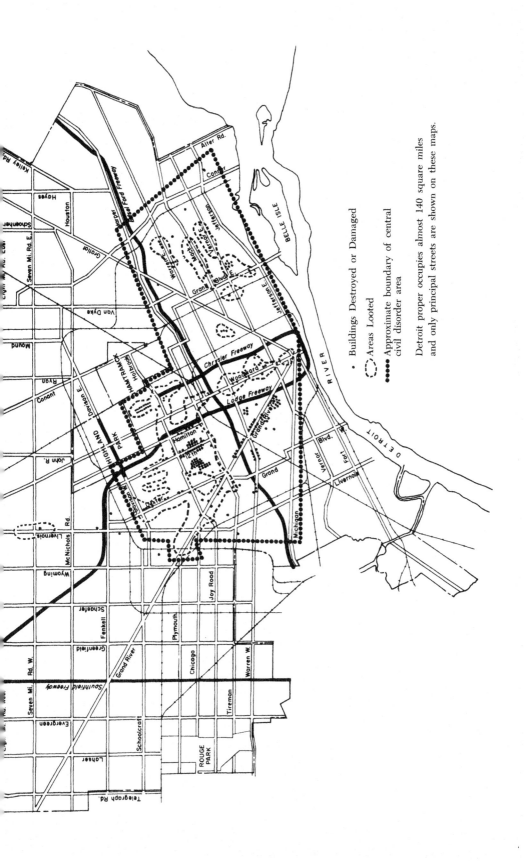

• Buildings Destroyed or Damaged

◯ Areas Looted

•••• Approximate boundary of central
civil disorder area

Detroit proper occupies almost 140 square miles
and only principal streets are shown on these maps.

Preface

The civil disorders that have erupted across the nation for the past five years have made painfully clear what many Americans have long feared. They indicate that race relations in the United States have reached the boiling point, that the cities of America are the arena in which the racial crisis will either be resolved or they will dissolve in a sea of social chaos, and that America has very little time left in which to find workable answers to this crisis if it hopes to survive.

Not all Americans, or even a majority for that matter, sense the racial crisis from this perspective or with this urgency, as the national response to the Kerner Commission Report has demonstrated. But for those who have lived through experiences such as that which occurred in Detroit in the summer of 1967, the future of urban America is a bleak one, unless this nation begins to take its cities seriously, and the black-white relations, which will to a considerable extent determine their future, as a matter of the highest national priority.

In essence that is why this book was written. It seeks to tell the story of the worst civil explosion that has taken place in any city in 20th century America: what happened, how, and to the extent that there are any answers, why. This book is, in a sense, deeply personal; it grew out of the desire, in fact the compelling urgency, of a life-long Detroiter who loves his city with all its grandeur and misery, whose career has been intimately related to Detroit in administrative posts in a university, in a civil rights organization, in the police department, and as a minister of one of the city's churches, to assess the experiences of July 23-31, 1967, and to find their significance for the nation's fifth largest city.

This book is necessarily, therefore, one man's opinion, subject to all the biases and limitations that such an effort obviously implies. It reflects, however, a deeply held conviction: that Detroit, and every other city in America is in a race with time—and thus far losing the battle.

Many persons read portions or all of the manuscript and made critical suggestions which were of invaluable assistance to the author. Their names are not mentioned, lest they be inadvertently associated with the interpretations made herein, but the author expresses silent and grateful appreciation to each of them.

Personal appreciation also is expressed to my secretaries who typed the manuscript, Mrs. Linda Higgins, Mrs. Florence Graves, Mrs. Helen Lacatis, and Miss Tina Lovio; to Mrs. Lois Pincus and the Reverend James Lyons, who diligently read proof copy; with especial appreciation to my Staff Assistant, Miss Janice Weiss, whose effort helped to make the manuscript readable, and last but certainly not least, to my wife, Jane, whose encouragement made this book possible.

H.G.L.

Prologue

A quarter century ago Gunnar Myrdal, the distinguished Swedish social economist and author of *An American Dilemma*, offered the cautiously optimistic judgment that "while the future looks fairly peaceful in the North, there are many signs of growing racial tensions in the South." "It seems almost probable," he wrote in 1942, "that unless drastic action is taken, severe race riots will break out in the South."

Myrdal's observations were made in his monumental study, undertaken at the request of the Carnegie Foundation, of what he termed America's "greatest failure"—the race problem in American society. His judgment about the future of riots was based on their noticeable decline in the period between World Wars I and II, and on the fact that, in his words, "they have become as unpopular as lynchings." Myrdal sounded a cautionary note about Detroit, however, which had experienced a clash between Negroes and whites in the spring of 1942 over the building of the Sojourner Truth Homes, a federally sponsored housing project in the northeastern section of the city. He described Detroit as being "almost unique among Northern cities for its large Southern-born population and for its Ku Klux Klan." With this exception noted, Myrdal quietly predicted that "on the whole, it does not seem likely that there will be further riots, of any significant degree of violence, in the North."

Less than a year after *An American Dilemma* (New York 1942) was published, Detroit erupted in the largest and most violent riot since the notorious clashes of Negroes and whites in Chicago and East St. Louis, Illinois, during and immediately after World War I. The 1943 riot in Detroit was a classic race riot which portrayed every major facet of Myrdal's riot typology. Whites mobbed and murdered Negroes in the downtown section of the city and the area west of Woodward avenue, adjacent to the downtown area, while Negroes on the city's east side pillaged shops, burned homes, and massacred those few whites who unwittingly found themselves in Detroit's "Black Bottom." The battle raged for less than two days, but when it was over, 10 whites and 24 Negroes were dead; 17 of the latter had been killed by police officers.

The experience of mass violence which broke out in Detroit 24 years later was on all counts more massive in its destruction than the 1943 riot, but infinitely more difficult to explain, both as to what happened and why it happened. How the 1943 riot started is still shrouded in mystery and rumor, but the 1967 riot can be chronicled almost by the minute. Why the 1943 riot erupted is a matter of elementary observation: for all practical purposes the city was a racial tinder box. Thousands of southern whites and Negroes had flooded into the city within a two-year period to compete for jobs in the war plants and for an already scarce supply of available housing. These southern immigrants had come to a city which, as Myrdal's observation reflects, was already renowned for its racial bigotry. Conversely, however, the 1967 riot occurred in a city which was riding the pinnacle of national acclaim as a model community in race relations in the United States. Why the worst civil disorder in 20th century America should erupt in such a city will remain a matter of debate for decades to come.

The 1943 Detroit upheaval, as previously noted, was a race riot in the classic sense of that term. Whatever the 1967 occurrence represented, it was not a race riot in which Negroes and whites battled each other in the streets. Most of the press insisted on calling the 1967 experience a race riot, and some police officers acted as though such was the case, but the facts are that the 1967 Detroit disorder was one of the most integrated events in recent history.

The aftermath of the 1943 riot saw the city make its first real, albeit feeble, attempt to make racial integration and social progress a matter of public policy. The effects of the 1967 upheaval have had the opposite impact; not only has there been a significant polarization of black-white attitudes in the city, but a growing sense of estrangement and separation even between the liberal elements in each group. The theme in the black community in Detroit is currently that of self-help and self-determination; in those areas of the white populace where the mood is not one of outright hostility and repression, there is a pronounced feeling that whites must support black efforts but avoid involvement in black affairs.

What all of this means for the future of Detroit is uncertain. There are simultaneously great possibilities and great dangers in the way in which the city is rebuilding itself, socially, economically and politically. But that is a matter for the future; this book is concerned with Detroit's recent past and to some extent its chaotic present. It is a record of a week of terror in the nation's fifth largest city, of the quarter century of agonizing progress and abysmal failure that preceded it, and of a tension-filled year of dramatic shifts in power alignments, political loyalties, and social perspectives that emerged in its wake. It is, in essence, the story of contemporary urban America, as seen in the racial struggles of one city, but a city whose success or failure may well hold the key to the future of urban life in the entire nation.

Persons Often Mentioned

After their initial and frequently summary introduction in the text, the following persons are usually referred to only by their surnames.

ALLEN, ROY A. Pastor, Chapel Hill Baptist Church; member, Detroit Commission on Community Relations; president, Council of Baptist Pastors; president, Detroit Council of Organizations.

BERTONI, ANTHONY. District inspector, Detroit Police Department; weekly duty officer, Sunday, July 23, 1967, when the riot erupted.

CAVANAGH, JEROME P. Mayor of Detroit since 1962; attorney and former president, National League of Cities; former president, U.S. Conference of Mayors; former vice president, American Municipal Association.

CLEAGE, ALBERT JR. Pastor, Shrine of the Black Madonna (formerly Central United Church of Christ); president, City-wide Citizens Action Committee; president, Federation for Self-Determination.

CONYERS, JOHN JR. U.S. congressman, 1st Michigan Congressional District (encompasses 12th street and the heart of the riot area), since 1964; attorney, and workmen's compensation referee in Detroit, 1961-64.

DIGGS, CHARLES C. JR. U.S. congressman, 13th Michigan Congressional District, since 1954; one of Detroit's two Negro congressmen (other is Conyers).

EDWARDS, GEORGE C. Judge, Sixth U.S. Circuit Court of Appeals, since 1963; Detroit police commissioner, 1962-63; justice, Michigan Supreme Court, 1956-62.

EMRICH, RICHARD S. M. Episcopal bishop of Michigan since 1948; chairman, Detroit Citizens Committee for Equal Opportunity, since 1963.

GIRARDIN, RAY. Detroit police commissioner, 1963-68; executive secretary to Mayor Cavanagh, 1962-63; chief probation officer, Recorder's Court (criminal court for the city of Detroit), 1961-62; reporter for the *Detroit Times*, 1929-60.

HOOD, NICHOLAS. Pastor, Plymouth Congregational Church, since 1958; Detroit councilman since 1965. (Hood and Melvin Jefferson, 12th street businessman and Hood's council campaign manager, alerted the author to the eruption on 12th street on Sunday morning, July 23, 1967, a few minutes after Conrad Mallett, former special assistant to Mayor Cavanagh, phoned that his son, a *Detroit Free Press* newsboy, had returned from a 12th street substation after a vain attempt to secure his Sunday papers!)

HUDSON, JOSEPH L. JR. President, the J. L. Hudson Company, Detroit's largest department store; chairman, New Detroit Committee, 1967 (succeeded by Max M. Fisher, September 1968).

JOHNSON, ARTHUR L. Deputy superintendent, Detroit Public Schools, since 1966; executive secretary, Detroit Branch, National Association for the Advancement of Colored People, 1950-64; deputy director, Michigan Civil Rights Commission, 1964-66.

KEITH, DAMON. Judge, U.S. District Court in Detroit; former senior member of the law firm of Keith, Conyers, Anderson, Brown and Wahls; co-chairman, Michigan Civil Rights Commission, 1964-67.

NICHOLS, JOHN F. Deputy superintendent, Detroit Police Department (now superintendent and first deputy commissioner).

PATRICK, WILLIAM T. JR. President, New Detroit Inc., since 1967; associate general counsel, Michigan Bell Telephone Company, 1964-67; Detroit councilman, 1957-64.

REUTER, EUGENE. Superintendent and first deputy commissioner, Detroit Police Department (now retired).

REUTHER, WALTER P. President, United Automobile Workers, since 1946; vice president, AFL-CIO, 1952-67.

ROMNEY, GEORGE. Secretary, U.S. Department of Housing and Urban Development; governor of Michigan, 1963-69; president, American Motors Corporation, 1954-62.

THROCKMORTON, JOHN L. Lieutenant general, U.S. Army; commander of federal troops (82nd Airborne Division) during Detroit riot.

VANCE, CYRUS R. Personal envoy of President Johnson to Detroit during civil disorder in 1967; deputy secretary of defense, 1963-67; presidential envoy to Greece during the Cyprus crisis, November 1967; U.S. representative to the Viet Nam peace talks in Paris with W. Averell Harriman, 1968.

WILLIAMS, G. MENNEN. Governor of Michigan, 1949-60; Assistant secretary of state for African affairs under the Kennedy administration; ambassador to the Philippines under the Johnson administration.

I
The Event

1. Detroit: July 23-31, 1967

Hope Disappointed

When the first of the nation's recent major civil disorders erupted in Harlem in the summer of 1964, a mood of apprehension spread through Detroit, as it did in many other cities in America. Was it an isolated occurrence or a sign of things to come? That question was soon answered as similar explosions erupted in urban ghettos along the eastern seaboard and then spread across the nation. During the next two summers, however, Detroit was somehow by-passed as urban rebellions erupted in Cleveland, swirled around America's fifth largest city, swept through Chicago and Omaha and out to the west coast, venting their fury on Los Angeles and San Francisco. As this occurred, Detroit's apprehension grew into a faint hope that perhaps it could be spared the experience of violence and destruction. In fact some Detroiters began to suggest that perhaps their city had found an antidote to riots in its progressive program of race relations.

In retrospect that hope proved to be futile and after the summer of 1967, in which Detroit experienced the worst civil disorder of any American city in the 20th century, many Detroiters began to console themselves with the feeling that a riot in Detroit had been inevitable—that it was only a matter of time until disaster struck. There had always been the fear, expressed by many after the fact, that if a riot erupted in Detroit, it would be one of massive proportions. Thus, prior to July 23 the mood of the city was one of uneasy confidence mixed with deepening dread; for three summers Detroit escaped the fate of every other major urban area in the nation, but if every other city had fallen victim to violence, how could Detroit avoid the same fate?

The city's anxiety was deepened in the early summer of 1967 by a drastic increase in the number of rumors of impending racial turmoil. These rumors, as a matter of daily routine, were sifted and investigated both by the city police department and by a special mayor's summer task force, created to coordinate a vast array of summer programs conducted by the municipal poverty agency, the department of parks and recreation, the public schools, and private agencies. Two rumors caused great concern to both the police department and the mayor's task force, and marked 12th street as an area of potential trouble.

The considerable amount of street prostitution on 12th street had long been a source of discontent for residents in the area and a focal point of resentment against the police. Residents complained bitterly about both the prostitution and the vice that accompanied it. They were convinced prostitution existed in part, if not primarily because the police consciously, perhaps even deliberately, allowed it to. The police, on the other hand, pointed to the difficulty of controlling prostitution within the strictures of the law. Arrests for "investigation as disorderly persons," traditionally effective devices for keeping prostitutes off the streets, had been discontinued by the police department in 1964 because they were blatantly unconstitutional. A newly enacted prostitution ordinance, passed by the common council at the police department's urging, was no sooner in effect and the first arrests made, than its constitutionality was challenged in the courts. Only a few weeks before the riot the state court of appeals ruled the ordinance unconstitutional.

In the interim the police department had adopted several

other strategies designed to cope with the problem. Following the insistence of many Negro citizens that the police place an equal burden of blame on the prostitute's clientele, the department took several steps to strongly discourage johns, most of whom were white and many of whom came from Detroit suburbs, from prowling in the ghetto. Potential customers attempting to flag girls from their cars, for example, became unwilling recipients of tickets for "creating an improper diversion" or blocking traffic. Men caught accosting prostitutes were subject to having their photographs taken by plainclothes officers carrying cameras with extraordinarily bright flash bulbs. Finally, in April 1967 and again responding to pressure, particularly from the 12th street community, the department assigned four integrated teams of foot patrolmen to walk 12th street from West Grand boulevard to Clairmount (precinct 10).* Within the first few weeks prostitutes began to disappear from the street corners. Almost simultaneously, however, a rumor began to circulate in the area that police officers had severely beaten a prostitute on 12th street, and as the story grew it came to include the pistol-whipping of her boy friend. Within a few weeks the rumor had gained such currency that it was being repeated as fact by well-known and respected people in the Negro community. In an attempt to obtain the facts, the police department sent teams of plainclothes officers from the citizens complaint bureau to scour 12th street. They sought names, place, date and time, or an eyewitness to the alleged assault. No one could supply tangible leads although everyone knew the story. Unable to find any substance to the rumor and noting it had sprung up at almost the same time foot patrolmen had been assigned to 12th street, police officials finally attributed the story to 12th street pimps or bar owners whose business had been rather drastically crippled by the presence of officers patrolling the area.

---

*Detroit police precinct numbers (1-16, no 3, 8, 9) are frequently cited herein to indicate the approximate position in the city of locations mentioned, at least by precinct areas, which are given on one of our maps. (Detroit proper occupies almost 140 square miles; because of the small scale of the maps, only certain principal streets appear on them.)

On Saturday evening, July 1, an incident of more serious proportions developed. A prostitute, well-known to police and in the community, was fatally shot at 12th and Blaine (precinct 10). Word spread quickly through the streets that she had been shot by two plainclothes officers from the vice squad. This story was eventually traced to another prostitute who had witnessed the killing and said the men involved in the shooting "talked like" vice squad officers. This witness also gave the story of yet another prostitute who allegedly observed the shooting and thought she recognized the assailants as two vice squad men who had arrested her several weeks earlier. Diligent investigation failed to produce this second witness, and although the murderers were not found, the assembled evidence seemed to indicate the prostitute had been shot by two 12th street musclemen who made their living by robbing prostitutes of their earnings. One of the presumed assailants was found stabbed to death on the same corner exactly one month after the riot.

Riot Erupts on the Sabbath Day

The Detroit riot of 1967 began with a routine raid on a well-known blind pig, chartered as the United Community League for Civic Action, on 12th street just north of Clairmount, at 3:45 a.m. on Sunday, July 23.° Twelve officers participated in the raid, four from the 10th precinct clean-up squad, a four-man precinct cruiser, and a squad patrolling 12th street. It was conducted after a Negro vice squad officer had gained entrance to the premises earlier in the evening and decided he could secure sufficient evidence to make arrests and a court case. Following a prearranged plan, the vice squad officer re-entered the prem-

---

°Blind pigs, illegal after-hours drinking places, were the social haunts of middle-class Negroes in the days when Detroit's hotels and nightclubs refused to serve them. As Negroes gained access to white entertainment spots throughout the city, the larger pigs lost their middle-class patrons and increasingly became the haunts of off-duty prostitutes, pimps, narcotics peddlers, and out-of-towners "looking for a little action."

ises at 3:35 a.m. The sergeant in charge of the clean-up crew then summoned a patrol wagon to expedite the transfer of prisoners. Ten minutes later the clean-up crew attempted to gain entry to the blind pig, was refused, and proceeded to force open the street entrance and a door on the second floor. For some reason, instead of the normal 30 or 40 persons usually netted in a blind pig raid, there were 82 on the premises that morning. Additional patrol cars were summoned, prisoners were loaded, and by the time the last wagon left the scene, a crowd of some 200 persons had gathered. In the crowd, according to police reports, were several persons who threatened the police and attempted to incite the crowd. The vice squad and clean-up officers knew that large crowds with a few openly hostile persons were common occurrences on such raids and did not, therefore, consider this an indication of potentially more serious trouble.

As the last prisoners were loaded, however, and the police cars began to leave the scene, bottles began to sail through the air from the rear of the crowd, one of which shattered the rear window of the precinct cruiser. With 82 prisoners in their custody, the officers quickly and properly left the scene.

The police department communications division records show that at 5 a.m. messages were being received and scout cars dispatched to runs such as "12th and Clairmount—man shot," "12th and Clairmount—officer needs help," "14th and Gladstone—trouble," "Linwood and Clairmount—all stores being broken into." Upon hearing these reports Raymond Good, lieutenant-in-charge at the 10th precinct, accompanied by Sergeant Lawrence Mulvihill, left the station and proceeded to 12th street. Enroute, Good heard a message over the police radio alerting all cars to stay out of the area. This message, coming sometime shortly after 5 a.m., was the first indication of serious trouble on 12th street.

At 12th and Clairmount, Good found several hundred persons on the street and sidewalks but observed no looting. He was not on the scene long, however, before a brick was thrown, striking him behind the ear. Good and Mulvihill left the scene, together with the Negro vice squad officer who had remained in the area after the raid. The latter reported that in the period between the completion of the raid and his departure, he had seen groups of young persons running through the area throwing objects and breaking windows.

Lieutenant Good then went to a police call box at Clairmount and the John Lodge expressway and notified Raymond Glinski, control center inspector, of the situation. Glinski in turn notified Inspector Anthony Bertoni, the weekly duty officer, and received instructions to secure sufficient cars from other precincts to quell the disturbance. Bertoni then called John F. Nichols, deputy superintendent, who set in motion the notification of all police department executives. Records show that Inspector Charles Gentry, commanding officer of the uniformed division on the west side of the city, was alerted at 5:15. Five minutes later Inspector Edward Mischnick, 10th precinct command officer, was notified. Gentry and Mischnick both arrived at the 10th precinct station at approximately 5:45.

By 6:15 a.m. Gentry had ordered immediate mobilization of all officers scheduled to work the day platoon in west side precincts. Mischnick mobilized the day shift at the 10th precinct and went to the initial staging area at Clairmount and the Lodge freeway, where officers were ordered to report as soon as they were notified. This area was quickly determined to be insufficient for the number of men and equipment that would be reporting, and the staging area was moved three blocks south to the rear of the Herman Kiefer Hospital—a spot that for the next eight days was known as Kiefer Command and became the hottest outpost of the riot period. That Sunday morning, however, as fast as officers reported, they were assigned to scout cars in teams of four and given immediate runs by the dispatcher at communications center. From the outset there were more runs to be made than cars available to make them.

Meanwhile, at police headquarters a different drama was unfolding. Police Commissioner Ray Girardin, who had been alerted at approximately 5:20, arrived at headquarters shortly before 6 a.m. By 6:35 most of the department's executives were on hand, and with preplanned precision the third floor of police headquarters was swiftly transformed from the offices of departmental executives into a headquarters command post. Ranking officers were assigned to predetermined units responsible for personnel, transportation, armaments, intelligence and communications. By 6:40 the tactical mobile and commando units from the motorcycle traffic bureau were mobilized. Two minutes later a teletype was issued by the deputy superintendent mobilizing all officers scheduled to report on the day platoon and ordering all men working at the time to remain on duty. By 7 a.m. the mayor and the state police were notified; at 7:07 the county sheriff's office was alerted; at 7:10 Colonel H. Dryden of the National Guard, the department's contact in the event of an emergency, was called. The police department log notes crisply, "Wife accepted information, Colonel at Grayling, Michigan." The significance of that call, and the information that Dryden was at National Guard training grounds at Camp Grayling, would not become fully apparent until later that day, when the guard was committed and the first contingent transported to Detroit from Camp Grayling, 200 miles and five hours away!

Between 7 and 9:30 a.m. all units of the police department were ordered mobilized, the FBI, prosecutor's office, fire and public works departments alerted, and all available policemen above the minimal requirements needed to secure the rest of the city were ordered into the 10th precinct. While these operations were being effected, a second strategy began to unfold on 12th street itself, one that had worked with considerable success in the Kercheval incident a year earlier, but would prove futile in this encounter.

A few minutes after arriving at police headquarters, Hubert Locke, Girardin's administrative assistant, telephoned the Reverend Robert Potts, rector of Grace Episcopal Church at 12th and Virginia Park, and president of the Virginia Park Rehabilitation Council, a federation of block clubs and civic groups in the 12th street area. By 8:30 a.m. Potts had assembled at the church over 20 well-known community leaders from the area, among them Julian Witherspoon, Robert Stott, and James Boyce of the Virginia Park Council, Congressman John Conyers, Arthur Johnson, deputy superintendent of schools, several 12th street businessmen, and pastors of churches in the community. Locke, who had visited the Kiefer command post in the meantime, arrived at Grace Church shortly before 9 a.m. and briefed the community leaders on the situation. Several phone calls were made to Girardin with reports on developments in the streets and observations of community leaders on the resources needed. It was finally decided that the community leaders would divide into four squads, canvass the area bounded by Woodrow Wilson, West Grand boulevard, 14th and Clairmount, and with the aid of bull horns try to persuade people to leave the streets. It was almost an hour before the horns arrived—another indication of the severe manpower shortage that Sunday morning. A car and driver had to be dispatched from headquarters to the police radio station on Belle Isle to get them, and then across the city to the disturbance area. During this time the situation continued to deteriorate. Police officers tried to cordon off streets leading into the trouble area but were hampered by the delay in getting sufficient barricades. When these finally arrived, there were not enough policemen to man them. Police squads attempted to sweep 12th street, using the traditional V-formation, but as the crowds, which by this time numbered in the thousands, dispersed in front of the marching squads, they quickly fanned through adjacent alleys to reassemble behind the policemen and pelt them with bottles.

It was 11 a.m. when the bull horns finally arrived and the squads of community leaders went into action. They were relatively successful in the southern end of the cordoned area, but as they converged on the intersection of 12th and Hazelwood, they met an entirely different situation. Here about 40 officers had retreated to a position two blocks in length, with one squad stationed at 12th and Hazelwood and the other at 12th and Clairmount. Within this area several fire trucks were battling the first of some 1,680 fires that would be set before the week was over. A crowd of approximately a thousand persons was standing in the street and on the sidewalk watching the excitement, while a much smaller group of perhaps a hundred, primarily young men, swarmed in the streets taunting police and firemen. It was into this area that Conyers, Johnson, Stott, and Locke drove. From the hood of Johnson's car Conyers and Stott tried desperately to persuade the crowd to disperse, only to have the small core of young men who had been taunting the police suddenly turn their attention and anger to those attempting to dissuade them from further disorder. One man climbed on the hood of the car and tried to wrestle the bull horn from Conyers, and others shouted wildly when he tried to speak. As TV cameramen moved in to take pictures of the scene, several bottles sailed through the air. Sensing their efforts would not work and acting on the tip from an acquaintance in the crowd that it would be personally dangerous to remain in the area, they left and notified police headquarters the situation was beyond control. Three busloads of police commandos assembled in formation on lower 12th street near Seward, having been pulled back pending the results of the community leaders' efforts, were pulled out of the area to await further reinforcements.

Fearing the situation would spread, police headquarters command began to beef up patrols in other sections of the city and to institute what was to become an agonizing process of securing outside help. Earlier that morning reconnaissance patrols had been assigned to Rouge Park and roadblock patrols had closed the Belle Isle bridge. At 11 a.m. police headquarters was placed under tight security. At 12:15 p.m. orders were issued by the director of personnel to guard all vital installations in the city. Acting on intelligence reports from 12th street informants, a select squad of knowledgeable and experienced Negro officers who knew the people and places of 12th street were given special assignments to work in the area. These men were later to be commended by Superintendent Eugene Reuter for the accuracy and speed of their intelligence reports from the field. As the hours passed, however, their reports grew increasingly grim.

It is questionable whether the carnival atmosphere, which according to the press prevailed on Sunday morning, actually existed in fact, but if it did, it did not last long. By Sunday afternoon the riot had taken on an increased intensity. At 2 p.m. came the terse announcement from headquarters command that Mayor Cavanagh, who had arrived there in the morning, had requested the assistance of 200 state troopers. At 3:05 word was received that 360 troopers were at the Eight Mile road armory awaiting transportation. At 4:20 p.m. Cavanagh requested the aid of National Guard troops, and by 5:25 p.m. the first contingent of guardsmen began to arrive at the Central High School staging area. Fifty minutes later Governor Romney authorized their activation, and by 6:57 guardsmen began to appear on Detroit's streets.°

At 4 p.m. police headquarters received a manpower report from Kiefer command that 156 policemen were committed to the trouble area, an additional 100 were detailed in squads of four to each barricade position, and 40 were being held in reserve. It was at this point, as the police were beginning to gain control of the 12th street situation, that the first confirmed report was received that crowds were forming on Linwood, three blocks west, and beginning to move north. This development marked the second phase of the riot that by nightfall would see looting and arson spread throughout the city.

For the next few hours, however, the path of the riot was westward. At 4 p.m. the first report of arson, at Grand River and Warren (precinct 2), was entered in the police log; at 5:05 came the first confirmed report of broken windows on Grand River; 20 minutes later reports of looting in the same area were being received. At 5:27 p.m. calls of breaking and entering, and looting were being received from the Seven Mile-Livernois area

---

°During the 12 hours between 7:10 a.m. when the National Guard was first alerted and 6:57 p.m. when they first appeared on the streets, a legally complicated and time-consuming process had taken place. The guard was mobilized, then formally requested by the mayor when it appeared the situation was beyond the ability of the local police to cope with, then formally committed by the governor, activated by the commanding general, and finally deployed on the streets. The two-hour period between the guard's commitment and deployment was partially spent in a dispute between its commanding officer and the head of the state police concerning under whose authority the guard would function after it was deployed.

1. A view along 12th street north of Clairmount on Sunday morning, July 23, about four hours after the riot began. The "Economy Printing" sign near the top center of the photograph marks the location of the blind pig whose raid by the Detroit police sparked the worst civil disorder in 20th century America.

2. Part of the throng on 12th street on Sunday morning, July 23.

3. Young people who were part of the crowds on 12th street on Sunday morning. They contributed significantly to what was termed the "carnival atmosphere" of the early hours of the riot.

4. Looking south on 12th street from Philadelphia street. The police officers in the foreground are protecting the firemen and equipment shown in photograph 1 (see also photograph 2).

(precinct 12); at 5:31 a confirmed report of 3,000 looters in the Oakland-Westminster-Owen area was logged, and at 5:44 a report of looting at John R. and Canfield, with the added notation that a police officer had been injured (precinct 13). The looting had moved to downtown Detroit 20 minutes later with reports of stores along Washington boulevard, Detroit's "avenue of fashions," being hit (precinct 1). In approximately an hour the looting had spread from 12th street and Linwood to areas covering over 25 square miles of the city.

At 7:45 p.m. Mayor Cavanagh issued a proclamation placing the city under curfew between 9 p.m. and 5 a.m. This proclamation was broadcast via police radio at 8:05, amid reports of continued looting and arson along Grand River, Warren, Livernois, Woodward, and Gratiot. Cavanagh had also given permission for a public announcement regarding the conditions on the streets to be made at Tiger Stadium, where the Detroit ball club was in the final innings of a double-header. An hour later came the report that two battalions of guardsmen were enroute to Detroit, 800 men from Grand Rapids and 800 from Flint. These men would be in Detroit less than 24 hours before word would be received of riot outbreaks in their own cities.

At 9:07 p.m. the first confirmed report of sniper fire, directed at the police helicopter, was received from the 1600-block of Seward (precinct 10). By 9:35 reports of sniper fire directed at firemen were received from the 12th-Lawrence-Collingwood area. During the same period a police teletype ordering all liquor establishments and theatres closed was dispatched. As this order was being carried out, the first of many similar reports that would be logged during the six days was broadcast over police radio, giving a west side location and warning that a gas station was "selling gas in buckets and bottles." At 10:25, on the request of Detroit Fire Chief Quinlan, Commissioner Girardin ordered all gas stations in the city closed.

During the next few hours the riot continued to grow in intensity. From 11 p.m. to midnight incidents of looting and arson were reported on an average of three per minute in an area covering 11 of the city's 13 police precincts. By the end of the first 19 hours of rioting, the police department had logged over 900 calls and scout car runs; over 10,000 people had surged through the streets of Detroit, looting stores in an area which extended from Livernois on the west to Conner on the east, and from the Detroit River to Seven Mile road. The police department had fought this battle with approximately 600 patrolmen on the streets for the first nine hours,° later augmented by some 350 state troopers, and finally, as the first 18 hours of the riot drew to a close, by approximately 900 guardsmen.

Over 300 fires had been set, with more than 40 still raging out of control. At one minute before midnight Governor Romney, who had arrived at police headquarters in the early afternoon, declared Detroit, Hamtramck, and Highland Park to be in a state of public emergency. But the worst was yet to come.

The Second Day, Monday

Under the governor's proclamation the mayor's curfew issued some four hours earlier was reaffirmed—all persons were to be off the streets between 9 p.m. and 5:30 a.m. No alcoholic beverages were to be sold or possessed. In addition, the proclamation ordered that "no person shall have in his possession any firearm or dangerous weapon, or any explosive or flammable liquid." In the aftermath of the riot it was discovered that Romney's legal advisors had neglected to attach appropriate penalties for violations of the proclamation; subsequently all arrests made under its provisions were thrown out by the courts. The proclamation did have the effect, however, of providing an authoritative basis for police action in dealing with the furor in the streets.

Shortly after midnight, July 24, Fire Chief Quinlan called for assistance from suburban fire departments. Within the next 72 hours over 90 pieces of fire equipment from suburban communities would respond, virtually stripping them of fire protection.

°At the height of the riot the police department had approximately 1,100 patrolmen available for street duty.

At 12:25 a.m. the first riot death was reported. In the light of subsequent interpretations, which primarily stressed Negro participation in the riot and made it appear that riot fatalities were the exclusive result of police action, it is significant that the first death was that of a 45-year-old white male who was shot by a white store owner, allegedly for looting. Within the next three hours two additional fatalities were reported; both victims were white. At 1:35 a.m. a 23-year-old white female enroute home with her family was shot at Woodward and Melbourne, apparently by a sniper (precinct 13). At 4 a.m. a 23-year-old white male was shot by guardsmen, allegedly for sniping, as he and several companions left the roof of their apartment building. His companions insisted they had gone to the roof only to protect their building from fires burning nearby.

Burning and looting continued throughout the night. In the short span of a single minute at 12:58 a.m., police cars were dispatched to 10 different locations on looting and arson runs. The appalling speed with which fires were devastating the city is reflected in three brief notations in the police log for the early hours of Monday morning. At 1:10 the log records a fire at Dexter and Davison; at 1:33 that entire block was on fire, and 19 minutes later the police communications center, which by this time had such a backlog of trouble runs that it was broadcasting information to any car in the area, was still vainly trying to get a car to the scene of the fire. As it happened, the whole block of some eight commercial establishments was gutted, including one of the city's leading Negro-owned apparel shops (precinct 10). Reports indicate that firemen at the scene were attacked by snipers and were preparing to withdraw when armed Negro homeowners in the area, alarmed lest the fire should spread to their residences, poured into the street to give protection to the firemen.

It was also during this period that the incredible story of appeals to Washington for federal troops first began to unfold. In the aftermath of the riot this episode was debated, disputed and decried, but very few facts emerged to shed light on precisely what took place. The facts are not very comforting, but they do reveal in a rather tragic fashion that would which is politics and government bureaucracy.

During the initial 18 hours of the riot, the Democratic mayor of Detroit and the Republican governor of Michigan managed to work together with rather remarkable effectiveness. Both had been on the scene since the early hours of the disorder, Cavanagh arriving at police headquarters shortly after 10 a.m., and Romney early Sunday afternoon. Cavanagh's requests for state assistance were acted upon with some promptness by Romney, avoiding the tragic mistakes in coordination between municipal and state offices made during the 1943 riot. Accordingly, a period of only a few hours elapsed between requests by the mayor for state troopers and guardsmen, and their commitment by the governor.

At 3 a.m. on July 24, Cavanagh and Romney announced they had requested that 5,000 federal troops be sent to Detroit. During the next several hours Governor Romney and U. S. Attorney General Ramsey Clark became embroiled in a controversy over precisely what kind of situation legally had to prevail in Detroit before federal troops could be committed. Romney was being advised by his legal staff to officially avoid any language in describing the Detroit disorder that could warrant the canceling of insurance coverage in the damaged areas. Clark, on the other hand, was working under federal statutes that limited the circumstances in which federal troops could be used—statutes that required the governor to declare the situation in precisely the language he was being advised to avoid. At 4:15 a.m., according to Cavanagh's subsequent testimony before the President's Advisory Committee on Civil Disorders, Romney announced he planned a revaluation of the request for federal troops with key people from the field before relaying his final official request to Washington. That request was not made until 8:30 a.m. when telegrams were dispatched to President Johnson and Clark recommending the immediate deployment of 5,000 federal troops.

Two hours later Romney made public a telegram from President Johnson acknowledging the request and indicating his willingness to send troops. Romney added that he expected the troops to arrive at Selfridge Air Force Base sometime in the afternoon. The troops did arrive, but they were preceded by Cyrus R. Vance, the president's personal envoy, who arrived at Selfridge field at 1:20 p.m. and was conveyed immediately to police head-quarters where he received briefings from Romney, Cavanagh, Girardin, Colonel Fred Davids, director of state police, and other officials. The briefings included the critical fact that all personnel resources of the city and state were committed, air reconnais-sance reports that 23 fires west and 6 east of Woodward were still burning out of control, reports that looting was still wide-spread throughout the city, and the urgency of having federal troops on the street before nightfall. Vance then left in a five-car convoy with Cavanagh, Romney, Conyers, and Michigan Attor-ney General Frank Kelley, to tour the riot area. Before leaving, however, Vance gave the group assembled for the briefings the unmistakable impression that he did not intend to commit the troops until later that evening when a more adequate assessment of the need for their deployment could be obtained.

Cavanagh and police officials were equally convinced that any delay in committing the troops would simply prolong the battle, especially if their presence was not visible throughout the city before nightfall. Accordingly, when the officials returned to po-lice headquarters shortly before 7 p.m. they were confronted with a group of some 40 Negro spokesmen from all parts of the city, including Congressman Charles Diggs Jr., Federal Judge-elect Damon Keith, 12th street businessmen, block club leaders, and church officials. With but one exception, they argued elo-quently for the immediate commitment of federal troops, insist-ing that the battle would become more intense after dark, and that if the city were to be spared further pillage and bloodshed, the visible presence of troops on the streets was essential.

Vance listened with apparent intentiveness throughout the meeting, but at its close announced that in his judgment federal troops were not needed at that point. Accompanied by Romney and Cavanagh, he then made the same announcement to the press. To the dismay of the Detroit officials, Romney voiced his agreement with Vance's decision. Noting he did not wish to ap-pear an inhospitable host, Cavanagh voiced his strong disagreement and once again made clear his judgment that the troops were needed immediately. His sentiments were also publicly backed in the news conference by Keith, co-chairman of the Michigan Civil Rights Commission. Emphatic in his insistence that Detroit was not experiencing a race riot, a fact many Negroes were beginning to feel the mass media were losing sight of, Keith stated there was an urgent and immediate need for federal troops on the streets of Detroit.

In Vance's behalf it can be said that the conditions on the streets of Detroit at 5 p.m. Monday would have led a casual observer to conclude the disorder had considerably subsided. Police and local officials who had lived with the riot since its inception, however, knew better, as did the people who lived in the affected communities. Following the news conference, therefore, a series of urgent phone calls took place between Cavanagh and community leaders, including Walter Reuther, UAW president, and between community leaders and the White House. One of the phone calls, which it is known went directly to the White House late that Monday evening, came from Reuther, who had kept in close touch with the situation throughout the day, both personally and through Mildred Jeffrey, UAW director of community relations and Democratic national committeewoman. Another call was made by Congressman Diggs, who had been on 12th street in the early hours of Sunday morning and had participated in the meeting with Vance. Which call or whose influence finally prevailed is unknown, but the commitment of federal troops was finally made from Washington at 11:20 p.m. The President then went before a nationwide telecast at midnight to announce his decision, and with thinly veiled slaps at Romney, to plead for a restoration of law and order in Detroit.

Earlier in the evening Vance had been persuaded to move the troops from Selfridge Air Force Base, some 35 miles from Detroit, to the prearranged staging area at the State Fairgrounds on the city's northern perimeter. Even so, by the time official word of commitment was received and the logistics of troop deployment determined, it was 1:10 a.m. Tuesday before federal troops appeared on Detroit's streets, 22 hours after the first request was made to Washington. Finally, and much to the surprise of local officials, General John Throckmorton, commander of the federal troops, announced that they would patrol only in sections of the city east of Woodward avenue, and that guardsmen, now federalized and under his command, would patrol west of Woodward. At no time during the week did the veteran combat-experienced men of the 82nd Airborne engage in action west of Woodward where the riot wrought its heaviest toll.

As this encounter between Detroit and Washington was moving to a climax on the third floor of police headquarters, a different drama was developing on the streets. A few minutes before 9 p.m. a message was broadcast that police were being fired on at Hillger and Charlevoix (precinct 5). At 9:04 word was received that a guardsman had been shot at this location. Eighteen minutes later the police radio made the terse announcement that a guardsman had been shot at Burns and Gratiot and was being taken to Detroit General Hospital. At 9:30 the report came of a wounded guardsman at Charlevoix and Lycaste (one block east of Hillger and probably the same incident reported at 9:04). Between 9:32 and 9:59, 13 separate reports of sniper activity in this east side area were broadcast; in 10 of these police or firemen were either pinned down by gunfire or believed to be wounded.

The next hour witnessed a running battle between policemen and snipers in this area. Large fires had been set at the intersections of Charlevoix and St. Aubin (precinct 7), Charlevoix and Hillger, and Gratiot and Fischer (precinct 5). At all three locations police and firemen encountered heavy sniper fire. At 10:15 policemen at the scene of the Gratiot-Fischer fire reported no sniper activity during the preceding 10 minutes, warned the fire was spreading, and requested the fire department to return to the scene. Four minutes later, however, from the Charlevoix-Hillger location came the report that state police were unable to pinpoint snipers and were pulling out because of heavy gunfire. Six minutes later firemen were reported under heavy sniper fire on Oakland between Clay and Hague in the city's north end, over five miles away (precinct 13). Between 10:55 and 11:02 three broadcasts were made for an ambulance to convey a wounded guardsman from Fairview and Goethe (Southeastern High School).

The height of the battle came between 11 p.m. and midnight. During this period two police precinct, two command post, and five fire stations were under attack by snipers. The police log for the hour reads as follows:

11:07   Livernois N. of Grand River; sniper cornered—may be in church tower [precinct 10]

11:12   St. Jean N. of Warren; fire house under heavy fire [precinct 5]

11:14   St. Jean N. of Mack; fire house under fire

11:30   St. Jean-Mack; firehall besieged, almost out of ammo [repeated, 11:31, 11:32]

11:35   St. Jean-Mack; firehall under attack

11:37   Firing at [precinct station] #7 from across street

11:41   Gratiot-Grandy, Mt. Elliott-Sylvester; both firehalls pinned down by snipers [precinct 7]
Crane-Brinket; fire at firehall [precinct 5]

11:45   Mack-St. Clair; sniper fire
Gratiot-Mack; small war, need help [precinct 7]
Jefferson-St. Jean; firing at rear of 5th precinct—all officers go in front door

11:46   Gratiot-Mack; officer and National Guard shot [repeated, 11:48]

11:47   Southeastern Command Post under fire [precinct 5]

11:48   Sniper fire on fire stations at Gratiot-Grandy, Mt. Elliott-Sylvester

11:50   Heavy sniper fire at Eastern High School Command Post [precinct 7]

11:51   Mack-St. Jean; fireman shot, need car in hurry [precinct 5]

11:52   Two wagons at #7 [ambulances sent to precinct station], officers shot

11:56   Mack-St. Jean; heavy fire [precinct 5]

12 M   Davison-Mt. Elliott; firehouse, heavy fire [precinct 11]

By midnight on the second day of the riot veteran police officers were convinced they were engaged in the worst encounter in urban guerilla warfare ever witnessed in the United States in the 20th century.

The Third Day, Tuesday

At midnight the battle still raged fiercely on the east side of the city, but shortly thereafter it began to subside and then shift with equal fierceness to Detroit's west side. Between 12:03 and 1 a.m., July 25, the police radio broadcast nine reports of sniper fire in the Mack-St. Jean area, including one order to halt all vehicular traffic on St. Jean between Warren and Mack (precinct 5). The first report at 12:03 was a call for an ambulance at Mack and Gladwin to convey a wounded civilian; six minutes later two persons were reported shot at that location, including one fireman. A minute later four police cars were reported under fire a block to the east, followed two minutes later by a none-too-subtle broadcast that "two white civilians" were shot at the Mack-Gladwin intersection and that one might be a fireman. At 12:20 came the terse announcement, "Mack and St. Jean—dead fireman."

As if signalling the tragic finale to the battle of the four preceding hours, the police radio reported three minutes later that firemen were pinned down by sniper fire at Linwood and Vicksburg, on the city's west side and roughly a quarter-mile from the scene of the riot's beginning point (precinct 10). In quick succession within the next three hours came 38 reports of sniper fire on Detroit's west side, and 11 on the east side. By 3 a.m. the sniper fire had suddenly diminished, with only two reports broadcast between 3 and 4 a.m., and no additional reports of gun snipers until almost 2 p.m.

During the daylight hours of Tuesday the major police activity was centered on closing gas stations that persisted in selling gas in defiance of the embargo, patrolling and making arrests in areas which were still being looted, accompanying fire equipment to the hundreds of fires still burning throughout the city, and beginning what was to become the massive operation of tracing down tips and anonymous reports on stored loot. The hysteria and vindictiveness of the citizenry was beginning to show also, as reflected in a police broadcast at 2.07 p.m. instructing cars in the Seven Mile-Westphalia area to investigate "a Negro male carrying a paper bag" (precinct 15), and one at 7:17 p.m. dispatching a car to a west side address for information on a sniper, with the dispatcher's comment, "female finking on husband." At 9:11 p.m. one of the city's well-known white extremists was reported to be barricading several streets with cars on the far east side of the city—for what purpose no one ever discovered.

It was also on Tuesday that the first in an enormous series of steps was launched to restore the city to a state of normalcy. At 8 a.m. Romney read a statement urging business to resume operations, jointly signed by himself, Cavanagh, and Vance. Two hours later he modified the emergency proclamation to permit the sale of gasoline between 12 noon and 5 p.m., limited to five gallons per customer and to be dispensed only into vehicle tanks. Bars and places of amusement remained officially closed, as did public schools on their own initiative.

The first of hundreds of prisoners still in detention were transferred under heavy security to Jackson prison shortly after 9 a.m. Later in the afternoon an additional 80 male prisoners were transferred to Jackson, 250 to the Ingham county jail, and 300 to the federal penitentiary at Milan. Police and military escorts were provided for public utility workmen in riot areas, while some state police units were sent from Detroit to outstate cities to assist in quelling disturbances which had arisen there the preceding night.

But the battle was not yet over. Sniper fire began shortly after 9 p.m. on the city's west side, near the original riot area. At 9:54 all police units were ordered off 12th street and seven minutes later were ordered to retreat from the area bounded by Woodrow Wilson, Dexter, Clairmount, and West Grand boulevard (precinct 10). During the next hour reports of police and guard patrol units under gun fire came in from eight locations scattered around the city. By 10:20 p.m. the curious pattern of the previous night's gun fire activity had begun to emerge again with a report of snipers firing on the Kiefer command post. Eighteen minutes later snipers were firing across Livernois into the 10th precinct station. Twenty-three minutes later snipers opened fire across town on the fire station at Mack and Rivard (precinct 1), 10 minutes later the fire station at Livernois and West Chicago, on the city's west side about half a mile south of the 10th precinct station, was under heavy sniper fire, and 19 minutes later the fire department command post at West Warren and Lawton came under sniper fire (precinct 2). In the last 25 minutes of Tuesday night, the police department logged 15 reports of sniper fire, 4 lootings, and 4 fire bomb incidents.

The Fourth Day, Wednesday

The early hours of Wednesday, July 26, turned out to be one of the worst periods of the riot. Of the 43 deaths occasioned by the riot, 7 were the result of incidents that took place during the first three hours of Wednesday morning.° Each of those incidents revealed tragic aspects of the riot; one became the most bizarre experience of the entire week.

The Harlan House Incident

At 12:46 a.m. the communications desk at police headquarters received a report that car 75 in the motor traffic division was under fire at the Lodge freeway and West Grand boulevard. The report, apparently made by officers in the besieged car, indicated

---

°Since it was sometimes difficult to determine which subsequent deaths were due to riot-sustained injuries, the exact number of riot-caused deaths became a matter of great confusion, but the police department now places it at 43.

that the direction of the sniper fire seemed to come from the roof of a two-story office building about two blocks southeast of their location. Four minutes later the police radio broadcast a report of snipers on the roof of the Burroughs office building on the west side of the freeway at the boulevard. Simultaneously, sniper fire was reported at Lincoln and Holden (precinct 2), approximately three blocks southwest of the original location. Eight minutes after the original report of sniper fire was received, the police department log shows the terse notation, "Harlan House Motel [east side of freeway], 4th floor—someone shot" (precinct 13). The victim was Helen Hall, 50, of Oakdale, Connecticut, who was in Detroit to inventory electrical supplies purchased by her firm. She had registered at the Harlan House on Sunday night, July 23. The *Detroit Free Press*, which has presumed to conduct its own homicide investigations of all the riot deaths, concluded that Mrs. Hall died from a guardsman's bullet. The police department homicide bureau's file carries the notation, "Case is open and investigation is continuing."

The Tanya Blanding Incident

Whether because of her age or the tragedy of the circumstances surrounding her death, the Tanya Blanding incident symbolizes the pathos a riot inflicts on those who are its hapless victims. Four years old at the time of her death, Tanya Blanding was huddled in the living room of a second floor apartment, a few steps from the intersection of 12th and Euclid, in the heart of the original riot area (precinct 10). Sporadic sniper fire had been reported in the immediate area earlier in the evening and on the previous night. Guardsmen reported one of their units under fire at the intersection and believed they had pinpointed it as coming from the apartment in which Tanya and her family lived. Precisely what occurred next is unclear; apparently as a guard tank was being moved into position directly in front of the building, one of the occupants of the Blanding apartment lit a cigarette. Guardsmen opened fire with rifles and the tank's .50-caliber machine gun. At 1:20 a.m. Tanya Blanding was dead.

The William Dalton Incident

There are as many versions concerning the death of 19-year-old William Dalton as there are persons to tell the story. The police log shows that shortly after midnight, specifically at 12:21 and 12:23, reports were broadcast that someone was breaking into a large moving and storage company warehouse at Grand River and Edmonton. Ten minutes later the warehouse was reported on fire and five minutes afterward the log carries a notation of sniper fire at the same location. What happened next depends on which story or witness one chooses to believe. According to one version, the police and guardsmen who arrived on the scene captured Dalton, ordered him to run, and then shot him as he fled. A second version recounts that as police arrived on the scene several youths, including Dalton, began to run in several directions, that the police ordered Dalton to halt and did not fire until he continued to flee. Dalton's body was found lying in the street at Grand River and Edmonton at 2:20 a.m. (precinct 6).

The Algiers Motel Incident

Within minutes of the initial breaking-and-entering report at the Grand River-Edmonton warehouse, the police radio reported a guard unit was under fire at Woodward and Euclid, some two miles away. The first broadcast came at 12:17 a.m. and was followed three minutes later by the radio report that state police were at the scene and were not in need of assistance. A few minutes later two similar reports were made. One indicated that someone was shooting at the house at 70 Virginia Park, a short block from the Woodward-Euclid intersection. The other re-

ported a sniper at Woodward and Euclid, and noted, "troopers
are there, no help needed." Both locations are just north of the
Algiers Motel, a long-time problem spot for police, frequented
by narcotics and prostitutes. (Two days earlier the police had
received tips that quantities of loot taken in the early hours of
the riot were being sold at the motel.) An entry in the police log
made at 2:21 a.m. reads, "8301 Woodward [Algiers Motel]—
check for dead person" (precinct 13). Sometime between these
brief entries three persons were shot to death in the motel annex
and seven other motel residents were beaten and abused.

The week following the riot at least five independent investigations of the Algiers Motel incident were underway; none however was as extensive as that of the police department itself.
When its investigation was completed, the department presented
its findings to William Cahalan, Wayne County prosecutor, who
issued first degree murder warrants against three Detroit police
officers, and several weeks later, conspiracy charges against a
private guard, one of the officers named in the original warrant,
and another police officer.

Both warrants were issued for only two of the three deaths.
The circumstances surrounding the third death, like many aspects
of the Algiers Motel incident, are clouded by a welter of con-
flicting testimony, although the evidence, including the testimony of both police and motel witnesses, points to the possibility that one of the three deaths occurred prior to the arrival
of the police. For those poised for charges of police brutality, the
Algiers incident became a horridly valid cause célèbre. For the
rest of the city, including many career officers in the police department, it was a disgusting moment in a tragic week. (See
John Hersey, *The Algiers Motel Incident*, New York 1968.)

The Larry Post Incident

Not all the deaths that occurred during those early morning
hours were of civilians. National Guard Sergeant Larry Post died
several weeks later of a gunshot wound in the stomach. He was

on duty with a guard unit at Dexter and Richton which fired on a car with three passengers who had ignored orders to halt (precinct 10). Who fired the fatal shot at 2:20 a.m. remains undisclosed, although evidence would indicate that Post fell in the crossfire that erupted in the attempt to halt the fleeing car. Post was one of two law enforcement officers and two firemen who lost their lives during the July riot.

Sniping Continues

As if the height of tragedy and senselessness had been reached in those early hours of Wednesday morning, the riot's intensity began to subside, and though it was not yet over, the battles became less fierce and less frequent. During those first few hours police had encountered heavy sniper fire on Glendale between 12th and Woodrow Wilson (precinct 10), approximately a mile north of the intense riot zone. Scattered gun fire and firebombing were reported throughout the city until dawn. From 4 a.m. until a few minutes before 3 p.m. there were only nine unconfirmed reports of gun fire. Most of the police runs during this period were to close bars and stores that continued to sell liquor, or to check out reports of stolen loot or breaking and entering.

At 2:55 p.m. a flurry of gun sniping suddenly erupted in several parts of the city. In rapid succession reports of snipers were received from the areas of Hamilton and Lawrence ("shooting at newsboys"), Leslie and Lawton ("woman wounded—need ambulance"), Livernois and Warren, Hazelwood and Second, the 2200-block of Blaine, Taylor and Woodrow Wilson ("man shot"), Woodward and Collingwood ("sniper on top of church"), and Clairmount and the Lodge freeway. An hour later the sniper fire again began to concentrate on police and fire department positions; between 3:55 and 4:09 p.m. reports from police and firemen under sniper fire were received from the area of Herbert and Livernois, Lee and Woodrow Wilson (just south of the Kiefer command post), and the 10th precinct station. There was also a report of an armed man in a house facing the Central

High School command post. Ninety minutes after it started the sniper activity stopped with equal suddenness and did not resume until after 9 p.m.

The riot activity after dark on Wednesday, however, was mild in comparison with the previous nights. Reports of police and fire units pinned down by sniper fire continued to come in, but without the fierceness of the preceding three nights. At 11:25 p.m. a police unit received a run to the 18,000-block of Hull in the northeast section of the city. The dispatcher's report was "baby stopped breathing." To that unknown family the situation undoubtedly had a terror all its own, but to veteran policemen who handle a dozen such emergencies every day, it was a sign that things were beginning to return to normal.

The Fifth Day, Thursday

Early Thursday morning, July 27, city, state, and federal officials turned their major attention to the gigantic health, food, and housing needs of the riot's victims, and began to lay plans for a long-term continuation of the emergency relief begun a few days earlier. A lessening of activity in the streets brought the nonpublic announcement from Vance that troops of the 82nd and 101st Airborne Divisions had been withdrawn to command post areas, leaving patrol responsibilities on the city's near east side to the 4th Infantry Division. State police were withdrawn from the city and ordered to resume regular duties. The problem of processing, transferring, and housing prisoners remained acute; at 9:30 a.m. the 13 police precinct stations alone held 1,671 prisoners in custody.

Shortly before noon Vance made a public announcement that he proposed to lift the curfew and restore gasoline service. The public reacted with a howl and the police department switchboard was flooded with calls of protest. How Vance could lift a ban imposed by the governor was unclear; however, the police log carries the notation, "7:15 p.m.—Curfew reimposed by Governor's office."

Events on the streets further illustrated graphically the many strange ingredients that were involved in the Detroit riot. Two factors stand out in the Thursday chronology: participation by whites and participation by out-of-towners. A few minutes after midnight two police officers in the 11th precinct had wounded a 24-year-old white male caught throwing a firebomb into a barber shop. Later in the afternoon police units engaged in a running gun battle with three carloads of white males in the Lodge freeway-Boston boulevard (precincts 13-10) area. The battle was short-lived and the police were able to apprehend one car and occupants. At 9:05 p.m. the police radio broadcast the description and license number (Kentucky plates) of a car occupied by three white males with shotguns. Besides the car with Kentucky plates, the police broadcast descriptions of cars with Alabama, California, Illinois, New York, and Ohio plates, all wanted for breaking and entering, possession of loot or guns, or firebombing.

Thursday was not without its comic relief, however. A frantic call from Detroit's model urban renewal community Lafayette Park, reporting "three suspicious colored men in a tan car," turned out to be three plainclothes Negro officers. And at 10:54 p.m. a desperate plea for help came from the 14,000-block of Santa Rosa—"Somebody stole her dog."

The Sixth Day, Friday

The hoped-for Friday calm was shattered a few minutes after midnight, July 28, by some two dozen hysterical calls reporting gun fire in a two-block area on Detroit's far northwest side. When police investigated it proved to be a family-trouble run. Reports continued throughout the day of cars with Alabama, Ohio, and Washington, D.C., license plates cruising the city.

Romney announced the state of emergency would continue through the weekend. During the afternoon, however, the gradual pull-back of troops continued—250 guardsmen were sent to Clark Park (precinct 4) and 750 to Northwestern Field (precinct 2), all on stand-by orders. It was announced the 82nd Airborne troops would be deployed Saturday from their command post at Southeastern High School to Chandler Park (precinct 15), to remain on stand-by until Tuesday. At 5 p.m. all police precincts were advised that Girardin had approved arrangements worked out during the day for clergy and civil rights commission staff to man precincts on an observer basis, a move necessitated by the increasing volume of complaints regarding the treatment of prisoners. At 8:15 p.m. the police department announced the availability of a prisoner information center at headquarters, culminating two frantic days of work by Inspector Henry Majeski and the staff of the liquor license bureau, tracing down the exact location of the more than 7,000 prisoners in the custody of the police or the county sheriff and lodged in some 20 different detention facilities throughout a six-county area!

The Seventh Day, Saturday

Saturday morning, July 29, the police department completed a major task that was not theirs to begin with, but was carried out by the staff of the street railways department under the able direction of Anthony Bertoni. Since Tuesday the department had undertaken the job, which properly belonged to the county sheriff, of finding detention facilities for the enormous number of post-arraignment arrestees, some of whom, for example, were temporarily quartered under guard on seven DSR busses, parked on a barricaded section of Macomb street, directly south of Recorder's Court. Girardin had personally arranged with Gus Harrison, state corrections commissioner, for the transfer of prisoners to Jackson and Ionia prisons; he gave to Bertoni the task of finding a sufficiently large and suitable detention facility closer to Detroit. After a prolonged process of fruitless negotiation with federal authorities for the use of the Fort Wayne military post and the exploration of such facilities as Brodhead Naval Armory and Cobo Hall, Bertoni turned to the women's bathhouse on Belle Isle. After its feasibility had been ascer-

tained, DSR crews worked on an around-the-clock basis, install-
ing floodlights and guard towers, ventilation fans, cots, and a
commissary. This facility, together with Romney's announcement at 11 a.m. that 1,400 prisoners, primarily curfew violators,
had been released five hours earlier, relieved the burden of
prisoner detention and enabled the sheriff to transfer all prisoners
being held in out-county facilities back to Detroit.

The Eighth Day, Sunday

By Sunday, July 30, the riot was over for all practical purposes.
Police units were still encountering isolated trouble spots but
most of their runs involved streets fights, family trouble, or loot
selling. The dispatcher's broadcasts reflected the break in tension; a few minutes after noon a scout car was sent to the city's
northwest area with the message "woman just shot her husband—
she missed." At 9:24 p.m. a scout car was sent to the State Fairgrounds area with orders to "protect the army boys; the girls are
after them."

The Ninth Day, Monday

Exactly when the riot officially ended is a matter of debate. The
army troops left the city on Sunday, July 30; curfew restrictions
were lifted on Tuesday, August 1; the perimeter around police
headquarters, the county jail, and recorder's court was removed
August 3; and the National Guard was demobilized the following
weekend. For the Detroit police officers who had been in the
thick of the battle since its inception, the end came when Eugene
Reuter, police superintendent, ordered the return to normal
eight-hour duty effective midnight, July 31.

It had been a costly battle: 43 dead, over 700 known injured,
some $50 million property damage, and an untold and incalcu-
lable loss in wages and tax revenues to the city. Detroit had just
been through the worst experience of urban violence in the
nation's history.

2. Detroit: 1943-1967

Remembrance of Things Twenty-Five Years Past

A small group of Negro agitators and another small group of white rabble-rousers are pushing this country closer and closer to an interracial explosion which may make the riots of the First World War and its aftermath seem mild by comparison . . . Unless saner counsels prevail we may have the worst internal clashes since Reconstruction, with hundreds, if not thousands, killed and amicable race relations set back for decades.

The irony of this statement is that it was not made in the aftermath of the riots that have swept across this nation during the past several summers. It is an observation by the well-known southern moderate Virginius Dabney, which appeared in the January 1943 issue of *Atlantic Monthly*, five months before a Detroit riot that took 34 lives. There may well be disagreement with Dabney about who is involved in the current situation; few, however, would argue with his prophetic judgment on what has been taking place.

A Model City

To understand Detroit and what took place in July 1967, it is important to examine at least the preceding quarter-century and the developments that, on one hand, made the nation's fifth largest city a most unlikely place for the worst civil disorder in the 20th century, and what, on the other, made such a disorder inevitable. By the mid-sixties Detroit was beginning to enjoy the reputation of being a model city in race relations in the North; in 1943 it was generally considered one of the nation's most segregated, if not bigoted, northern cities. With the exception of the automobile plants, whose practices had been influenced both by unionism and by World War II, Detroit in 1943 was a closed society for Negroes. They were clustered in four residential areas. The greatest concentration was found on the lower east side in a section called Black Bottom (in precinct 1 and SW precinct 7), which ran north from the river, merged into notorious Paradise Valley, with Hastings street (now partially replaced by Chrysler freeway) as its commercial, entertainment, vice-ridden center, and finally terminated in a section known as North End (both in precinct 13). A second, smaller but more stable cluster lived on the city's near west side, an area of modest, single family residences with a significantly high proportion of home owners (in precinct 6). A third enclave had developed after World War I in Highland Park just west of Hamilton (and into precinct 10); and the fourth, in Detroit's northeast section, was a surprisingly well-integrated area called Conant Gardens (in precinct 11). This latter area, however, was the scene of a major racial disturbance over a public housing project in 1943 (now Sojourner Truth Homes), which to some extent helped to touch off the 1943 riot. While these four black pockets were not all slums, few Negroes lived outside their boundaries, and nothing happened to change this situation until the 1948 United States Supreme Court decision on restrictive covenants, which was based in part on a Detroit case. It was this decision which for the first time opened significant portions of the Detroit housing market to Negroes.

Until after World War II, in addition to the residential segregation, Detroit's major hotels, restaurants, nightclubs, and legitimate theatres either were closed to Negroes or relegated them to separate areas. It was 1948 before Negroes were given overnight accommodations in Detroit's largest downtown hotel, and even later before they were admitted to the decent and some not-so-decent restaurants. During this period none of the large churches of famed Piety Hill accepted Negro members, the YMCA allowed Negroes only in the "colored" branch, and even taverns and restaurants on the edge of the Wayne State University campus refused to serve Negroes as late as the mid-fifties. And while the factories and foundries of the automotive industry were integrated, their white collar staffs were not. Outside these factories, Negroes worked in department stores as bootblacks and elevator operators, and in banks and office buildings they swept floors or served as porters. Those who were fortunate enough to obtain college degrees and did not enter one of the four traditional Negro professions—law, medicine, teaching, or the ministry—found federal post office jobs.

Race Riot: 1943

Perhaps the most significant symbol of 1943 Detroit was its police department, generally credited at that time with being one of the most bigoted in the North. The ranks of police officers were swelled by an exceptionally high number of white southerners, while the less than two percent of the force who were Negroes were generally assigned to only two precincts, either the old Hunt street station, which patrolled Black Bottom, or the Canfield station, which handled Paradise Valley. During this period Negro police officers were frequently reprimanded for arresting white persons; stories abounded during the 1943 riot of police officers who aided white mobs assaulting Negro victims or stood by and watched. The attitude of police officers and officials was perhaps the most volatile municipal issue for Detroit's Negroes in the post-war era.

In such an atmosphere, aggravated to the boiling point by massive numbers of southern blacks and whites who poured into Detroit during the early months of World War II seeking lucrative defense plant jobs but competing for an already scarce supply of housing, the 1943 riot was inevitable. Like the upheaval that would occur almost 25 years later, it began on a sultry summer Sunday, sparked by a rumor which began on Belle Isle, one of the city's most frequented public parks. When the rumor reached white ears, it contained that classic motif of white anxiety—a Negro had raped a white woman. The story which spread to black residents in Paradise Valley alleged that a white sailor had thrown a black baby into the Detroit River from the Belle Isle bridge. Neither story was ever found to have any basis in fact.

The battle raged for two days and nights—June 20 and 21. It was marked by incredible scenes of mob violence as crowds surged through downtown Detroit, mercilessly setting upon any hapless victim in sight. Negroes were dragged from streetcars and beaten into a stupor while whites were attacked by black mobs with equal fierceness. In an almost ironic forecast of the 1967 disorder, the city was not restored to some degree of normalcy until Tuesday when federal troops were sent at the governor's request to occupy the city. In the wake of the disaster were 34 dead, over 500 injured, and 1,800 arrests. (See Alfred McC. Lee and Norman D. Humphrey, *Race Riot*, New York 1943.)

In the aftermath of the 1943 riot Mayor Edward Jeffries appointed Detroit's first interracial committee. This step, together with the persistent work of the Detroit Branch-NAACP, the Urban League, and a number of other organizations, began slowly but perceptibly to break the back of racial segregation in Detroit. It was as though the 1943 riot awakened the city to the fact that its black populace had to be reckoned with; Detroit began to move in ways and on fronts where it had not moved before. After 1948 Negroes began to rent or buy homes throughout most of the city; by the late fifties segregation in places of public accommodation had all but disappeared. In 1957 William Patrick Jr. became the first Negro elected to the common council, while better jobs in the public utility, banking and mercantile industries were opened to Negroes, though not without hard-fought battles, in some instances even into the sixties.

Five years after the 1943 riot G. Mennen Williams was elected governor. His 14-year administration as Michigan's chief executive had a significant impact on the racial climate of Detroit. Through his appointments he first gave Detroit a succession of Negro judges, all but one of whom won re-election at the polls. Williams also kept his 1948 campaign pledge to secure the enactment of a fair employment practices ordinance; it was six years before he won its passage in a rural- and Republican-controlled state legislature, but the statute and its implementing commission became major factors in expanding new job opportunities for Negroes in the fifties. Williams won deep loyalties in Detroit's Negro community, loyalties that would still be visible in 1966 when Williams found himself locked in battle with Detroit's popular young mayor for the Democratic nomination for U.S. senator.

A Young New Mayor

It was in the present decade, however, that the most dramatic action began to develop. In spite of the movement in other areas, very little had transpired to change the attitude of law enforcement agencies, and in the winter of 1960 this became a cause célèbre in Detroit's Negro community. A series of attacks upon white persons by Negroes reached an emotional peak in Detroit when a white nurse was fatally assaulted by a young Negro, a few blocks from one of the city's major hospitals. It resulted in the announcement of a police crackdown by Mayor Louis Miriani, and although he later denied he intended Negroes to be its victims, the police unquestionably got that impression. The series of wholesale arrests and indiscriminate street interrogations and friskings which followed created such an outcry in the Negro community that in the next election Miriani was defeated, along with a member of the common council who was outspoken in her racial antipathies. The defeated mayor was replaced by Jerome P. Cavanagh, a young and virtually unknown 33-year-old lawyer making his first bid for public office, and the councilwoman was replaced by Mel J. Ravitz, an epitome of liberalism and a Wayne State University professor of sociology. What had begun as a hostile protest vote ended in a startling victory for Detroit's Negroes who had not realized their own political strength but whose efforts succeeded in setting the stage for a new chapter in Detroit's history.

The election of Cavanagh was highly significant for several reasons. Not only was Detroit in trouble racially at the time of his election, it was also in deep difficulty economically and culturally as well. One of Cavanagh's first appointments was that of Alfred Pelham, a prominent Detroit Negro fiscal expert, as city controller. This not only gave the Negro community reason to feel that the new mayor had not forgotten those to whom in large measure he owed his election, but also brought acknowledged expertise to the city's crumbling financial situation. Cavanagh and Pelham devised the city's first income tax, which began to reduce the huge municipal debt and restore fiscal integrity to the city's operation. Negroes also suddenly began to appear at municipal "state" functions, a factor not important in itself except that it set a climate for communication and social discourse between the city's Negro and white citizens. An exciting bi-racial team of aggressive young Detroiters was put together by the mayor and they began to tackle with zest the problems of industrial development, urban blight and decay, racial tensions, and a staggering list of other municipal problems. The nation's overgrown Midwest farm town slowly and painfully began to move into the 20th century.

His First Police Commissioner

The most significant of Cavanagh's early actions, however, was the appointment of his first police commisioner. In a move that even the most knowledgeable in the Negro community did not anticipate, he persuaded George C. Edwards, a state supreme court justice, to resign to head the police department. Edwards was one of the few white persons in Detroit held in high esteem by the Negro community. With a background in labor organizing in the thirities, and having served as judge of the city's juvenile court, and as a member and subsequently president of the common council, Edwards had earned a reputation as a flaming white liberal in the days when "white liberal" was still a badge of honor. An almost audible sigh of relief went through the Negro community when his appointment was announced; it was considered the first major breakthrough in the volatile area of police-community relations.

Edwards set in motion a series of reforms within the department, designed in his words to "build a bridge" between the police and the people. His accomplishments must be measured in the light of the times; Edwards was the first commissioner in the department's history to take the historic tensions between the Negro community and the police seriously. In spite of his major commitment to this problem, it was only one of many in the police department in 1962. The task Edwards faced was that of charting a totally new direction for one of society's most tradition-bound institutions, renowned for its resistance to change. Nevertheless, he created the first meaningful police-community relations bureau and made the first in what would become a series of promotions of veteran Negro officers, including the first Negro inspector. Under his leadership the explosive problem of protection for Negro families moving into white residential areas became a matter of firm police policy. After two years in office, Edwards was appointed judge of the Sixth U.S. Circuit Court of Appeals by President John F. Kennedy.

A New Police Commissioner

Edwards' successor as police commissioner was, like Cavanagh himself at the time of his election, virtually unknown in the Negro community. Those who knew him best, however, predicted he would revolutionize law enforcement. The word in town was that Ray Girardin "knew where the bodies were buried." A native Detroiter, Girardin had been a top reporter for the *Detroit Times* for over thirty years. He had written and sometimes solved many of the big police stories that broke in Detroit from the prohibition era until the *Times* folded in 1958. His next post was chief of the probation division of Recorder's Court, from which he was tapped by Cavanagh to become his executive secretary in 1962. As quasi-deputy mayor, Girardin guided Cavanagh through the early days of his administration and a close personal relationship developed between the two. Consequently it was somewhat natural for Cavanagh to place Girardin in the enormously taxing and politically sensitive post of police commissioner.

Girardin's chief advantage over his predecessor lay, ironically, in the fact that he had the same rigorously liberal philosophy but without the public reputation as a crusader. Those who knew him also knew that in temperament and commitment he could well have been a founding father of the American Civil Liberties Union, though unlike Edwards he had not been in the public spotlight. Veteran police officers accepted him as one who had solved more murders as a crime reporter than the homicide bureau and was basically "on their side." The Negro community adopted a wait-and-see stance but did not wait long before they saw just where the new police commissioner stood.

One of Girardin's first moves was to abolish the ancient police practices of investigative arrests and tip-over raids. Both were blatantly unconstitutional and Girardin publicly said so, but both practices also were tender spots in the Negro community. Investigative arrests permitted police officers to hold primarily prostitutes in custody overnight without preferring charges. In spite of its validity as an enforcement-control mechanism, the practice had degenerated to the point that any suspicious person could be and was arrested and locked up, only to be released the following morning without being formally charged with the commission of a crime. Tip-over raids, likewise, began as an effective albeit illegal way of controlling the operation of blind pigs and gambling houses; the police simply battered their way into a suspicious location, and without benefit of a search warrant or other judicially acceptable evidence, proceeded to search the premises, lock up occupants, and destroy everything that might in their judgment be used in a vice operation. On behalf of the police and those segments of the Negro community whose neighborhoods were infested by after-hours drinking and gambling operations, it must be said that the tip-over raid was a relatively effective way of limiting such activity. The problem was, as it is in many aspects of law enforcement operations and procedures, one of discretion, and in this instance far too many Negroes enjoying a quiet game of poker and a few drinks in their homes with friends found themselves the object of tip-over raids with all the resultant destruction and embarrassment.

Following a series of conferences with civil rights organizations and the city commission on community relations, Girardin also made drastic changes in the operation of the departmental citizens complaint bureau. Charged with the responsibility of receiving and investigating complaints concerning mistreatment by police officers, the bureau's effectiveness had been hamstrung by the arduous route its reports traveled from the time they left the bureau until they arrived, in those few cases they actually did arrive, on the commissioner's desk. Girardin placed the bureau directly under his personal command and then moved its operations from police headquarters to rented space in the downtown YMCA so that, as he put it, "citizens would not have to walk into the lion's den to complain about the lions." He then promoted and placed a Negro sergeant in the recruiting office and gave clear orders to make the recruitment of Negroes a matter of priority for the entire recruiting staff. Girardin also placed the full weight of his office behind the development of monthly meetings in police precincts between citizens and precinct commanders, where local problems of law enforcement and community relations could be dealt with on a continuing basis. In a series of carefully planned promotions and assignments, he uncovered a cadre of young professional but virtually buried police officers, and moved them into the forefront of the department's command and administrative functions.

During the day Girardin was always in his office at police headquarters, personally directing every phase of the department's vast and intricate operations. At night he took to the streets and was often at the scene of a serious crime before the first scout car arrived. He became so well-known in the Negro community that rank and file citizens would stop him in the street for a chat. His personal presence on the scene of tense situations in the city prevented several near-explosions that could have occurred prior to 1967.

The Citizens Committee for Equal Opportunity

The progress that marked the six-year period before the July 1967 riot was not of a steady or even quality. While there were signs which on the surface gave reason for hope for Detroit, at a more profound level they were a portent of deep feeling and unresolved concern. In June 1963 a tremendous march of a quarter-million Detroiters, both Negro and white, took place on a warm Sunday afternoon along Woodward avenue, the city's main thoroughfare. A great deal of anxiety concerning the march built up in the city several days before hand; many saw it as calculated to produce trouble. The fact that it transpired peacefully allayed those fears and many subsequently came to see it as a great and dramatic expression of solidarity regarding the plight of Negroes in the South. The march, known as the Walk to Freedom, was led by Martin Luther King Jr., Cavanagh, Reuther, and other national and local leaders. That it was tranquil however, and that it magnificently achieved its stated objective of demonstrating the concern of northern Negroes and whites for the racial struggle in the South, did not blind Detroit's white leadership to the fact that more intensive movement on racial justice and equality would have to take place in Detroit as well. Even before the march, groundwork had been laid for the creation of the Citizens Committee for Equal Opportunity. The brainchild of Walter Reuther, it was chaired by Episcopal Bishop Richard S. Emrich, and included in its highly selective membership the top decision makers in Detroit business, industrial, labor, educational, judicial, civil rights, religious, and civic affairs. The stated aims of the committee were to mobilize the broadest possible leadership in the city, to place its influence behind the goal of equal opportunity in education, employment, housing and public accommodations, and to achieve equal justice in law enforcement for all Detroit citizens. The committee attacked the morass of racial problems in the city; some of its most notable work was in the area of police-community relations where, under the driving leadership of Horace Gilmore, circuit court judge, significant accomplishments were made in accelerating the recruitment of Negroes and establishing continuing education and in-service training programs for police officers.

Conservative Reaction

The social changes thus taking place in the city produced an inevitable conservative response. There were rumblings from white homeowner groups that the mayor and police commissioner had become captives of "special interest" civil rights groups, and several white extremist factions began to emerge and become vocal. They found a cause in 1965 when William T. Patrick, the lone Negro member of the city council, resigned after six years in office to accept a legal position with the Michigan Bell Telephone Company. A special election was called in the fall to fill the vacancy, and the conservatives found their leader in Thomas Poindexter, a local attorney who had become an enthusiastic but exceedingly inept champion of homeowners' rights. He rode to power on a petition-referendum drive to make the right to practice racial discrimination in housing a city ordinance. Both the petition and the subsequent ordinance were innocuously worded, so much so that the ordinance was eventually ruled unconstitutional. But its intent was clear, it received enough support to be approved by a narrow margin, and Poindexter was elected to the common council. In the next councilmanic election Poindexter lost to the Reverend Nicholas Hood, minister of one of Detroit's largest Negro churches, but he made a rapid recovery and managed to win election to Recorder's Court.

The election in which Poindexter was defeated and Hood elected involved several factors forecasting a new mood developing within Detroit's Negro community. The election of John Conyers as Detroit's second Negro congressman in 1964 had signaled a break in the old political alliance between labor and the Negro community; Conyers had run with strong backing from the Negro clergy and with local union support, but without the blessing of Solidarity House (UAW). He won nomination, which in his district was tantamount to election, by the narrow margin of 43 votes on a recount. Two years later in the fall primary when the votes for common council candidates were tallied, it became clear that Negroes had voted heavily for a bi-racial slate, while the votes from white wards chiefly showed support for only white candidates. Even before the primary the Reverend Albert Cleage Jr., who was considered a political and ecclesiastical renegade by most of his fellow Negro clerics and was also a candidate for common council, had been urging a vote-black campaign. After the primary Negro pastors reluctantly but firmly announced that the segregated white vote gave them no alternative but to urge their parishioners to vote only for Negro candidates. Liberal sentiment in the white community responded. Led by the Citizens Committee and the mass media, a massive campaign was mounted to persuade white voters to vote a bi-racial slate. The outcome was the election of Hood, but it also marked the deepening disillusionment in Detroit's Negro community with the efficacy of the ballot in the civil rights struggle, just five years after the discovery of how potent the vote could be in that struggle.

The Riots Move Westward

While Detroit was engaged in this period of political, economic and social readjustment, other metropolitan centers around the nation began to explode. Detroiters became apprehensive in the summer of 1964, many of them remembering the tragedy of 1943. As the east coast riots of Harlem, Bedford-Stuyvesant, and Trenton began to move westward into Philadelphia and Rochester, Detroit began an intensive campaign to avert the holocaust. The police department dispatched special observers to each riot city, and on the basis of their observations, prepared a special riot manual to be followed in case of a local outbreak. Careful liaison plans were worked out with the state police and the National Guard in order to avoid the costly error of 1943, when some 15 hours elapsed before state law enforcement assistance was received. The Mayor's Total Action Against Poverty program went into high gear, and together with the public school system and private agencies, launched an impressive array of special summer projects to provide employment and educational, cultural, and recreational programs for the city's youth. The United Community Services, representing private social agencies, made a special appropriation for Operation Sweep (summer week end emergency project) to give member agencies funds to expand their summer staffs and programs. The Citizens Committee, which served as a prod to public and private agencies, contributed the idea of a special cadre of teenage youths engaged in remunerative non-technical police duties, under police officer and citizen supervision. Headed by Robert Potts, former police youth bureau inspector, this became one of the most highly praised and effective programs for teenagers anywhere in the nation.

As the riots during the summers of 1965 and 1966 hit Cleveland, miraculously by-passed Detroit, and swept westward to Chicago, Omaha, Los Angeles and San Francisco, Detroiters began to feel that perhaps they had discovered an antidote for violence. In the aftermath of the 1967 riot, those who had worked diligently to keep Detroit from exploding would be accused of complacently assuming it could not happen in their city, but during those four years no one in any position of responsibility expressed such a naive opinion. On the contrary, it was precisely because many citizens, both Negro and white, knew that Detroit could erupt that they worked with such persistence. Repeatedly the mayor and civic leaders insisted they were working not simply to avoid violence, but more important, to erase the inequities in jobs, housing, education, and law enforcement that barred

5. A view of Linwood avenue looking south from Joy road on Sunday afternoon, July 23. Fires such as this were raging out of control at three separate locations in the city.

6. Looting during the Detroit riot, as this photograph from the 2nd police precinct indicates, was a well-integrated affair.

7. Detroit police officers dressed in full riot gear guard firemen and equipment at one of the numerous locations where fires were set during the riot.

8. National Guardsmen at old Eastern High School, East Grand boulevard and Mack, one of several staging areas for troops throughout the city.

growing segments of the populace from full first-class citizenship.

As one might expect, Detroit's efforts and its avoidance of an eruption did not go unnoticed by the rest of the nation. The nation's fifth largest city became the symbol of hope for national news and magazine articles on the problems of big cities. Teams of social scientists began to probe and analyze Detroit's many and varied urban and social renewal programs. The city became the prime example of a working, effective poverty program for federal agency heads in Washington. The U.S. Department of Justice made grants available to law enforcement agencies around the nation to study model police programs and operations. Detroit was chosen as an exemplary city in police-community relations. Not all the commentaries on Detroit were favorable; an exhaustive study of United Foundation supported social agencies by Greenleigh Associates made penetrating criticisms of the middle-class structure and orientation of a significant number of agency programs. But even this study, locally requested and financed, could be seen as the mature, introspective aim of a city that was aware of its own shortcomings to do a more thorough, effective job of serving its citizens.

The Kercheval Incident

On August 9, 1966, Detroit had a minor eruption which tended to confirm the nation's faith in its future. On a warm Tuesday evening a police cruiser got into an altercation with a group of young Negroes loitering on an east side street corner. A half-hour later the cars of white persons traveling through the area were stoned and gangs, primarily of youths, began to appear on street corners. Within minutes the area was cordoned off and squads of riot-trained police commandos were sweeping the streets. A citizens' group in the predominantly Negro community swung into action with a telephone campaign to block-club presidents, urging them to squelch rumors and advise their neighbors to keep youngsters off the streets. The few fires that were set were quickly extinguished, looting was confined to less than six stores, and an effective police intelligence operation apprehended a car containing a small arsenal and members of the Afro-American Youth Movement. It had been followed from the heart of the riot area across the city, and was finally stopped on the west side, three blocks east of 12th street.

On the second night of what came to be known as the Kercheval Incident, a summer rain began to fall about 9 p.m. and it was all over. With the generous assistance of Divine Providence, the Detroit police had quelled a riot in its infancy without firing a single weapon, with no loss of life, and with a minimum amount of destruction. Coming in the wake of the disasters in Cleveland and Chicago, Detroit rose even higher in the nation's estimation; no one realized how quickly the successful handling of the Kercheval incident would be forgotten a year later.

A Young Old Mayor

The twelve months preceding the 1967 riot, however, opened on an ominous note, the Kercheval incident notwithstanding. Cavanagh was defeated in a hard-fought battle to wrest the Democratic nomination for U.S. senator from G. Mennen Williams. The 1966 fall election stirred many pockets of controversy in the city, from those who thought Cavanagh had not kept faith with the mandate given him in his two to one reelection victory as mayor a year earlier, to those who were piqued with him for challenging the Democratic party machinery, which had thrown its support to Williams. The Negro community was divided over the Cavanagh-Williams battle; even many Negroes who supported Cavanagh felt that he had been and would continue to be the key to the city's progress and that Detroit could ill-afford to lose him as mayor.

Cavanagh's defeat signalled the beginning of a concerted attack on his administration by the city's conservative forces. Although he had taken a vacation to do his state-wide campaigning, his absence from the city left him open to the charge of neglecting municipal affairs. The chief municipal problem to hang around his neck was obviously that of crime, which had been soaring in every metropolitan community, and in Detroit long before Cavanagh decided to make his bid for the U.S. Senate. Nevertheless, crime in the streets, a key campaign issue in Cavanagh's mayoralty race of a year earlier, was resurrected, only this time the political assault was led by Mary Beck, Detroit's lone councilwoman. Her repeated criticisms of the mayor and his administration finally evolved into a Cavanagh-recall movement, which was still floundering when the July riot broke.

Forced to adopt a defensive posture for the first time in his six-year career, Cavanagh found himself in the spring of 1967 fighting a woman's scorn on one hand, and announcing to municipal employees that Detroit faced an austerity budget for the coming fiscal year on the other. A two-day city-wide crime conference called by Cavanagh diverted the crime issue temporarily into more constructive channels, but the budget problem then moved into the forefront. The news that there would be no salary increases triggered a revolt by the city's 3,300 patrolmen who, for the first time in their careers, were engaged in collective bargaining with the city. Attempts to persuade Cavanagh to reconsider the salary issue finally led to a slowdown in writing traffic tickets, which delighted the public but left the mayor less than overjoyed. The patrolmen, led by their police officers association and guided by one of Detroit's top labor attorneys, countered next with a sick-strike, euphemistically dubbed the "blue flu incident." Almost one-third of the patrolmen failed to report for duty and the police department was on the verge of calling in the National Guard to patrol the streets when the intervention of the Citizens Committee for Equal Opportunity brought a cessation of hostilities. A pact calling for a cooling-off period and a fact-finding procedure was hammered out by Edward L. Cushman, Wayne State University vice president and labor expert, Richard Cross, attorney and board chairman of American Motors Corporation, George Bushnell, attorney for the public school board, Father Paul Harbrecht, dean of the

University of Detroit Law School, and the Reverend James Chambers, one of the city's key Negro clerics. The pact was agreed to on June 10, barely six weeks before the riot.

"The Urban Challenge"

Perhaps the most thorough and objective look at Detroit and where it stood on the eve of the July riot was unintentionally provided by the *Detroit News* in a series of articles entitled, "The Urban Challenge—Can the Cities Survive?" The culmination of six months of intensive research comparing Detroit with its four big city neighbors—Cleveland, Indianapolis, Chicago, and Milwaukee—it was the work of Jerome Aumente, a perceptive young *News* reporter. He, too, found that observers around the nation were focusing on Detroit as an "action city," successfully responding to the challenge of survival, and wrote:

> In many ways metropolitan Detroit is beginning to piece together the workings for a grand scheme of urban development. There is a Detroit Regional Planning Commission, a Forum for Detroit Area Metropolitan Goals, a Greater Detroit Hospital Council, a federal Transportation and Land Use Study, a Huron-Clinton Metropolitan Authority for parks and recreational areas, and a county pollution control system. In many of these things it is far ahead of other urban areas.

On the critical area of race Aumente observed:

> As in other large cities, Detroit's most pressing urban problem lies in the persistence of the Negro ghetto . . . But despite its racial difficulties, Detroit is seen as being closer to a solution than other large urban areas. It enjoys a reputation in the Great Lakes area of a willingness, at least, to search out solutions . . . Complaints in other cities range from hostile Negro-police relations to intractable school boards. Detroit has heard these, too, but its progress in answering them has brought reporters from as far away as Los Angeles and London, England, to take a look-see . . . Though to Negroes in the city, the schools are the

first on their agenda of complaints, the educational system here is noticeably better than in other major cities. Similarly, while crime looms large as a problem for Detroit, ranking high among the Mayor's dilemmas, it is no higher here than in other major cities . . . But if Detroit stands out from the others in its police image, it is because of the growing rapport between citizen groups, principally Negro, in the inner city core and the police precincts.

Aumente's summary article, which included the above observations, appeared in the Sunday, May 28, issue of the *News*. Exactly two months later Detroit would explode in the worst experience of urban violence in the 20th century. Aumente had documented the fact that Detroit was seen as "being closer to a solution" of its racial problems than other major urban areas. Close, perhaps, but not close enough.

3. Riot Response: The Police and the Courts

Were the Police Firm Enough?

By 7 a.m. on July 23, 1967, two platoons of police officers, each consisting of a sergeant and 11 patrolmen, had been dispatched to 12th street with orders to clear the streets. The sergeants in command of the platoons made a decision upon their arrival at the scene which was confirmed several hours later at police headquarters. That decision became one of the most bitterly contested aspects of the riot and was the subject of endless debate thereafter. In brief, the issue was, and to many still is, whether police action was firm enough at the outset.

Many citizens, both Negro and white, were outraged that the police did not take firmer action. The *Michigan Chronicle*, the most widely circulated Negro weekly in Detroit, headlined its July 29 issue, "It Could Have Been Stopped!" and entitled its lead story, "Did Police Just Write Off 12th?" The story itself quoted the paper's editor that police were "just standing around" while looting took place and carried his observation that "if police had stopped looting when it was centered on one 12th street block early Sunday when the mood was allowed to become a 'Roman Holiday,' the riot could have been prevented."

The editorial, however, drew widespread criticism. In a front page editorial the following week, the *Chronicle* pointedly noted that the call for firmer police action was not a recommendation that police "should use undue force or shoot to kill." However, in spite of the *Chronicle*'s subsequent moderation of its position, a great many Detroiters felt the police action on 12th street that morning was wholly inadequate and inappropriate.

What the appropriate and adequate police action might have been, no one has ever been willing or able to suggest, although in the confusion of that first day, all sorts of advice was given, from using police dogs (which the department does not have) to using fire hoses. The latter suggestion came from a prominent and militant civil rights leader, to whom it was explained that in addition to potentially triggering an outrage as great as that experienced when the infamous Bull Conner used the same technique in Birmingham, Alabama, the pressure from fire hoses would have left a carnage of broken bones and battered skulls lying in the street.

For the two sergeants who were first on the scene, the issue of appropriate police action was less dramatic but crystal clear. Both men are quite explicit in saying that at the time of their assignment, their orders were neither to shoot nor to refrain from shooting looters; they were to use whatever force was deemed necessary to quell the disturbance. As they recount the scene after their arrival, they describe crowds of well over 1,000 people on the street, many standing on the sidewalks watching, while others darted in and out of broken store windows or doors. To have used firearms in that situation, they insist, would have inevitably meant the risk of shooting young children and women with infants in their arms. The police officers did attempt to clear the streets and they did make arrests, but they did not shoot. Those who were there at the time have no regrets about their decision—they can sleep with their consciences at night!

Later that morning Girardin supported his officers' decision before a group of community leaders who met in his office. He stated firmly that while the department would employ every legitimate means at its disposal to quell the disturbance, it would consider the value of human life above that of property and would accordingly seek to restrain the rioters with a minimum loss of life. It was undoubtedly one of the most humane judgments ever made by a police official in the midst of such a civil disturbance, but in a society as materialistic and as property-oriented as is America, the response to it was understandably and tragically appalling. The post-riot critics—"armchair generals" as they came to be called at police headquarters—never quite found a comfortable way to quarrel with the commissioner's judgment. After all, who would say publicly that property is worth more than human life! When, however, Girardin later reiterated his stand in an article in the *Saturday Evening Post* of September 23, 1967, the *Detroit Free Press* launched a screeching preview editorial attack on September 13. In the *Post* article Girardin said that "any riot can be crushed. But this would be an invitation to revolution." To this the *Free Press* responded:

> *It would not . . .* of course any riot can be crushed and of course any riot must be crushed and beyond this, any potential riot ought to be nipped in the bud, and still beyond this, conditions which provide the climate for a riot ought to be quickly changed.
>
> The alternatives of crushing a riot and causing a revolution, or not crushing a riot and permitting widespread destruction may be Mr. Girardin's alternatives but they are not ours. Laws must be enforced. Implicit permission for lawbreaking, the sort of permission which Mr. Girardin's police force gave Detroit's looters in the early hours of our disturbance, produces just what was produced here—widespread lawbreaking and escalating lawbreaking to more serious crimes.
>
> Nor does there need to be any choice between shooting child looters and permitting massive looting, another false alternative Mr. Girardin set up in his article. Reasonable and sufficient force to maintain law must be applied . . . Negroes and whites alike have a right to expect official assurances that their persons and their property will be protected.

What constitutes "reasonable and sufficient force" was never made clear, either by the *Free Press* or anyone else. Most of the critics failed to grasp the significance of one basic fact. When the riot began on Sunday morning, 311 police officers were on duty in Detroit, of which 193 were on street patrol. The headquarters command post activity log records that shortly after 5 a.m. Anthony Bertoni, weekly duty officer responsible for command decisions during the afternoon and midnight platoons, gave instructions to the control center inspector to secure sufficient cars from other precincts to quell the disorder. As it turned out, those cars were involved in a near-frantic response to an incredible number of calls that began to pour into police headquarters around 5 a.m.—"12th and Clairmount—man shot," "14th and Gladstone—trouble," "12th and Clairmount—officer needs help," "Linwood and Clairmount—all stores being broken into." By the time executives in the department had been alerted and mobilization orders given, the crowds on 12th street were already numbering in the hundreds. Unlike the Kercheval incident of a year earlier, there simply was not a sufficient number of police personnel available to respond in force.

The reason for the tragically small complement of men available that Sunday morning is simple. For more than a year the police department had repeatedly indicated that it was over 500 men short of its authorized strength. As it entered the summer of 1967 the department had slightly over 3,300 patrolmen, to be divided into three platoons (shifts), distributed among 13 precincts and 12 bureaus, and then reduced by some 40 percent to allow for furloughs and leave or sick days during July and August. Finally, for every two police officers on street duty, another one is required for support assignments, such as communications or prisoner processing and detention. Furthermore, the period from 4 a.m. Sunday to Monday morning is usually the quietest one in the week as far as crime and law enforcement are concerned. And although the public may not believe it, police officers share the same human needs common to the rest of the citizenry; although they are theoretically on duty seven days a week, they enjoy days off (leave days), go to church, and have families they like to take to the beach or the cottage or camping. And that happens to be where a number of off-duty Detroit police officers were on Sunday morning, July 23—at early Mass or at the beach or spending the weekend at the cottage. The simple truth is that Sunday morning, from a police perspective, is a bad time to have a riot.

The manpower situation on Sunday, July 23, also accounted for one of the basic differences between the police response that morning as contrasted with the highly lauded police action during the Kercheval incident a year earlier. The Kercheval incident had erupted on the sultry night of August 9, a few minutes after eight. An unusually large force of police officers was on the streets of Detroit that night. The incident broke during the third platoon when police strength, because of traditional crime patterns, is at its highest. In addition, not only had the tactical mobile unit just come on duty an hour before—in ironic contrast with the 12th street raid when it had just gone off duty an hour before the riot began—there was also an "End the Viet Nam War" rally at Central Methodist Church in downtown Detroit. Such rallies frequently were targets of a group of right-wing extremists in the city and were therefore potential places of conflict. A special unit of police officers stationed near the church in case trouble arose, became the first contingent dispatched to Kercheval street when the alert was given.

The other principal difference between the Kercheval incident and the 12th street riot was the type of conflict situation the police faced. Kercheval was primarily a teenage disturbance, consisting of relatively small crowds of youths whose primary activity was limited to pelting passing cars with bricks and tossing poorly-made molotov cocktails, most of which never ignited. In contrast, 12th street was a man's war—the participants were much older, and right from the start the crowds were incredibly larger. Once it was underway the 12th street riot became an awesome experience of widespread well-accomplished arson and gun sniper activity. Neither the police nor anyone else, however, had any indication at the outset that the pattern of the 12th street riot would be any different from that of the Kercheval incident, except that the crowds were larger and the available police strength smaller. The police strategy that had worked so well a year earlier and was providentially assisted by a generous summer rain on the second night, proved futile on 12th street. There also lingers the suspicion in the minds of some, whether any type of police action on 12th street, given the nature of the disturbance, would have been effective.

Some citizens also harbor the suspicion that a series of internal difficulties in the police department might have contributed to a low morale among the patrolmen and consequently resulted in a markedly slow response of police officers to the mobilization orders issued shortly after 6 a.m. on July 23. There is ample evidence that the department had been through an incredible two-year period prior to the riot; veteran officers describe it as the worst two years in their careers. It had been under intensive scrutiny by two Wayne County grand juries, whose efforts were sparked by a conviction, fanned by the press, that a major scandal of bribery and corruption existed in the department. The personnel problem had also begun to take on serious dimensions, with more men resigning, primarily for economic reasons, than could be replaced by new recruits. Simultaneously, the crime problem was beginning to attract major attention among the citizenry, with "crime in the streets" becoming the most frequently discussed and debated issue in town. This in turn had brought on the inevitable political feuds, which mounted to an intensity sufficient to spawn a recall movement against the mayor and a demand for the firing of the police commissioner. The Kercheval incident also, while successfully handled, was simply an added strain on an already tense, undermanned, overtaxed department. Finally, the spiraling wage scale in Detroit had triggered a demand by the Detroit Police Officers Association for significant salary increases in a fiscal period when all indications were that the city budget would incur its first sizable deficit in several years. The inability of the city and the officers association to resolve this dispute had led to the blue flu incident. The department was just beginning to recover from this when the riot broke.

What effect all of this had on the police response to the riot, no one really knows, but available evidence would suggest it was relatively insignificant. No officer failed to report for duty when called, and once on the job, many men worked three and four hours beyond their required 12-hour shifts. Many are the stories of men who became ill or were injured but reported back for duty without medical permission. Ironically, after the blue flu incident police officers, half-jokingly reflecting on the series of crises the department had just undergone, frequently expressed the opinion that matters had to get better because they could not conceivably be any worse. That opinion, of course, died swiftly on the morning of July 23.

The Administration of Justice

Of the many problems that arose during the riot, none was greater than the detention of the 7,800 persons arrested from July 23 to 31, and their processing through that maze which is the administration of justice in American society. As many persons were arrested and processed through the courts in six days as were processed in six months under normal circumstances. In contrast to the police, however, who at least during the first three days were somewhat uniformly praised for their action, the courts and those responsible for prisoner detention facilities came under almost immediate fire and were accused of having suspended the Constitution by exacting excessive punitive measures against those arrested. Unlike the criticism of the police, which developed in the later stages and aftermath of the riot, and came from people who were hostile toward or outraged by police action but in most instances had little if any technical or personal knowledge and experience on which to base that criticism, the critics of the courts came from the ranks of the legal profession itself: the bar associations, the dean of one of the city's three major law schools, and the American Civil Liberties Union.

If the courts did not respond to the riot within the best tradition of American jurisprudence, at least it must be acknowledged on their behalf that the juridical situation they confronted would have put even the best of court systems to the test. At the outset of the riot the criminal court was opened around the clock, and though most judges worked for only six-hour shifts, at least the mechanism for speedy arraignments was provided. To some observers, however, that mechanism was far too speedy. On Tuesday, July 25, the dean of the University of Detroit Law School assembled a volunteer staff of attorneys to assist the Neighborhood Legal Services Center, an arm of the city's poverty program, in providing legal counsel for arrestees at the time of arraignment. These attorneys concentrated initially on interviewing and the arraignment-bail release process for female prisoners who had been abruptly separated from families and children. It was considered to be both humane and of minimal risk to the continuance of the riot to assist them to return to their families as soon as possible.

Initially a number of judges apparently decided it would be in the best interests of restoring law and order to prevent arrested rioters from returning to the streets too easily. With one exception, therefore, they uniformly set bonds ranging from $10,000 to $200,000. This, in turn, meant not only the temporary detainment of prisoners until their arraignment, but also the problem of detention after arraignment, technically under the jurisdiction of the county sheriff. The county jail was filled to capacity within 36 hours. At one point the jail, which has a maximum capacity of some 1,200, was crammed with over 2,200 arrestees. But it fell to the police department to make hasty arrangements for transporting prisoners and detaining them at six other penal facilities in the state, including the state prisons at Jackson and Ionia, the federal penitentiary at Milan, and county jails in Monroe, Washtenaw, and Ingham Counties. When these were filled to capacity, with the aid of the Detroit Department of Street Railways, the police department hastily converted the women's bathhouse on Belle Isle, one of the city's largest parks, into a detention center. Because of its pleasant situation on an island in the Detroit River and its rather comfortable appointments when compared to most county jails, the police and prisoners quickly dubbed it Belcatras. A number of inmates inquired if they could serve out their entire sentences within its walls.

The American Civil Liberties Union

By far the sharpest criticism of the criminal court was directed at its judicial posture during the riot. To many attorneys it became an extension of the police department; rather than being an independent arbiter of guilt or innocence, exercising judgment upon police decisions and practices, often the court seemed to assume the guilt of those brought before it and used high bond as a security measure in a way not consistent with its purpose. In a number of cases prisoners were arraigned *en masse* and in several instances only after some judicially intemperate remarks were made from the bench. By Wednesday, July 26, the Detroit branch of the American Civil Liberties Union had become sufficiently alarmed to convene an extraordinary session of its executive board which unanimously issued on the following day a statement calling for certain actions to be taken immediately "to remedy some of the injustices that have inevitably occurred as a result of the impossible burdens to which our police and our courts have been subjected."

Viewed in retrospect, the statement was remarkably restrained in its criticism of the police. The courts, however, did not escape so easily. In part the statement read:

> In calling for remedial measures, the Metropolitan Detroit Branch of the ACLU wishes to place no blame upon any of our city officials who, on the whole, have served the public interest with remarkable devotion. At the same time the constitutional rights of those who have been accused of participating in the rioting cannot be left unattended if we are to restore the respect for law and order which has broken down so completely in the last week. Order has apparently been restored. It is essential that law be restored as well. The first was fundamentally the job of the police and the military, the second is the primary responsibility of the courts.

Persons arrested have almost without exception been held under excessive bond without respect for their personal circumstances or the nature of the charges against them. Attorneys have been unable to talk to their clients, in part because of the confusion and chaos which has existed, but also because certain public officials have not been diligent in making this possible.

Normal facilities for obtaining information to enable the courts to make a reasonable and individual evaluation of the circumstances of the accused have been totally inadequate to deal effectively with the massive problems presented to them.

The normal system of assignment of counsel by the court for indigent persons has been inadequate to meet the demands of the situation. Even the listing of the names of persons in custody and the location of their places of confinement has been beyond the scope of the available resources. To the extent that these and other breakdowns in the system are the result of a shortage of judicial manpower, the standby offer of the Wayne Circuit Bench to assist the Recorder's (i.e., criminal) Court made last Monday . . . should be accepted and implemented immediately.

The ACLU statement then recommended a number of specific steps to remedy the situation, including an immediate inventory of the names and locations of all arrestees; an acceptance by the court of assistance offered by public agencies concerned with securing information for the purpose of setting reasonable bonds; a review of bonds already set; access by attorneys to all persons in custody; the early release of female prisoners; the request and acceptance by the juvenile court of assistance from social workers and community agencies; and the disqualification of judges who had engaged in prejudicial conduct on the bench.

In spite of its harshness, the statement reflected a sensitivity to the strain the police and the courts were placed under during Detroit's episode of America's "summer madness." If the riot demonstrated anything at all in this area, it reflected how fragile are the restraints that hold a social order together and how even the majesty of the law can break down in an appalling fashion in the midst of such a massive civil crisis.

4. Riot Response: The Mass Media

News Blackout

Any catastrophe tends to reveal the best and the worst in people and institutions. The Detroit riot was no exception. This was true of the police and the courts; it was equally true of hospitals, churches and bar associations, businesses, colleges and universities.° Perhaps no segment of the community revealed this schizophrenic reaction to the disaster and its aftermath more clearly than did the mass media.

Viewed from one perspective, the general policies of the press and television were commendable, and the actions of their staffs heroic. Shortly after the riot began Judge-elect Damon Keith, one of the first Negro citizens to arrive at police headquarters, after a hasty consultation with Girardin, phoned Martin Hayden, editor of the *Detroit News*. With Hayden's assistance Keith secured an informal agreement from the mass media to delay making public reports of the riot until the police had had an opportunity to control the situation. The agreement was honored by the major local media with the result that residents of other

---

°Several private Detroit hospitals accepted injured law enforcement officers but would not accept riot victims.

cities knew about the disturbance before many Detroiters did.

Reporting the Agony

When the self-imposed news blackout was lifted early Sunday afternoon, many reporters and cameramen took to the streets with the same professional dedication that sent police and firemen into the battle-areas. They had a job to do and were determined to do it to the best of their ability. Some did so at great personal risk to their own lives and safety; many probed diligently beneath the surface to uncover interesting, revealing, and sometimes bizarre information that helped to put the many-faceted aspects of the Detroit riot into better focus.

Some of the editorial comments that appeared in the local and national press during this period were extremely noteworthy. Six days before the Detroit explosion, on Sunday, July 18, 1967, the *Detroit News* ran a lead editorial whose title, "Newark's Lesson—We've All Failed," indicated its sensitive content. The editorial described in poignant phrases the "failure of our American society to digest its Negro minority" and "the ghettos [which] bear witness to that failure"—"the walls [of] today's Negro ghettos [which] are higher and harder" and the need for "so much more in money, perception, imagination" to deal with ghetto problems.

One of the most perceptive commentaries on the riot, however, appeared in the *New York Times* of July 27, four days after the disorder began. Entitled, "The Agony of Detroit," this editorial outlined some of the developments that had marked racial progress in the city and gave "grounds for hope that Detroit could escape Newark's fate." "Why then Detroit?" the editorial asked. In response to its own query, the *Times* made a pertinent observation which the Detroit papers would repeatedly fail to grasp:

For one thing, the agony of Detroit cannot be laid to the early restraint of the city's well-disciplined police, as some observers—Negro as well as white—have suggested. If the police had shot

81

their way in at the first sign of trouble, they would unquestionably have provoked the same kind of violent reaction and bitter recrimination that have followed strong police intervention in Newark and elsewhere. The fact that heavy violence occurred anyway does not disprove the point. If Detroit shows anything in this regard, it is that the police are damned if they do and damned if they don't.

After also repudiating those who would "write off the violence in Detroit as merely the work of the arsonists, looters, murderers, and other lawless elements," the *Times* editorial drew two conclusions from the events "that have condemned forward-looking Detroit to the fate of less-deserving cities."

> One is, that if Detroit is an example of America's best efforts to solve the racial and other problems confronting its cities, the best is not nearly good enough. The other is, that even if progress is achieved on a broad front, the United States must be prepared to contend with serious turbulence in the cities for a long time to come.

Even now, months after the riot, these two observations stand out as one of the wisest and most realistic appraisals of the Detroit disturbance.

Reporter Fatigue?

If the performance of the mass media merits commendation on one hand, it deserves chiding if not condemnation on the other. It is impossible to know whether the same battle fatigue that afflicted policemen and firemen also affected newsmen, or whether the local media were incapable of displaying the same objective sensitivity to the violence that erupted in Detroit as they had to the violence in other cities. For whatever reason, there were occasions when the activities of the media were extremely disconcerting to many in Detroit who were in the thick of battle.

In spite of the voluntary moratorium on news and telecasts, many reporters and cameramen were out on 12th street on Sunday morning shortly after the riot began. Some stayed discreetly on the sidelines or behind police barricades; others, lugging cameras and equipment, waded into the midst of the crowds, attempting on-the-spot interviews, and were determined to be wherever the action was next. Disturbingly, the action developed wherever the news cameras went; both policemen and citizens on the street reported that wherever a camera moved, a flurry of excitement began, especially if the lens was pointed at a group of youths. Time and again police officers had to leave their positions to rescue some cameraman who had become isolated by the crowds from his crew or discovered his car and equipment had been parked in an area into which the rioters subsequently moved.

And if the *Detroit News* was praiseworthy in its interpretation of the Newark riot, less than a week later it had forgotten its own sound judgment. On July 24, the day after the Detroit riot began, the *News* carried a front-page editorial entitled, "The Senseless Few." The difference in tone between the two editorials was astonishing. Negroes in the ghetto who had been so sensitively described in the July 18 Newark editorial as "in confinement, spatial and social [where] employment is a burning grievance [and] housing a corrosive sore," became in the July 24 Detroit commentary "mobsters, arsonists and looters" in neighborhoods that "do not teem with unemployment." The editorial went on to assert that "times are not desperate in Detroit for people who want and can work and the rioters who rampaged were not confined to the unemployed." Aside from the tacit suggestion that those who are unemployed are those who do not want to work, the editorial's inaccuracy concerning the state of employment in the city was surprising. Economists had been predicting a setback in Detroit's economic picture for well over a year; automobile production was down from the previous year; and an effort by the Citizens Committee which persuaded Detroit businesses and industries to hold a one-day job-recruitment fair in the 12th street area, only six blocks from where the riot later erupted, had produced over 3,500 job-seekers in less than six hours. This was barely two months before the riot began.

The July 24 editorial was correct in some of its assertions, especially in pointing to the difference in racial climate in the city between 1943 and 1967. But its most serious error was its attempt to put in perspective what was taking place in the streets by saying:

> And yet it happened here.
> That doesn't prove that all the efforts of a quarter-century have been in vain. A few hundred or a few thousand Negroes have shown their contempt for law and the system; a half-million others stayed out of it, hoping and waiting with their white fellow citizens for the rampage to end and the rule of law to be restored.

By the time this editorial appeared on the streets of Detroit, three people had already died in the riot. All were white. One had been shot as a looter and one as a suspected sniper. Scores of whites were already in custody for looting or other offenses, and yet not only this editorial, but the media in general persisted in describing the occurrence as a "Negro riot" throughout the remainder of the week and for days thereafter. Somewhat curious, also, was the fact that in this editorial, whose general tenor sought to support the Negro community, "negro" was spelled twice with a small *N*. It was the first time in years that Detroit's Negroes had seen this grammatical or typographical slip in the public press, but it would occur with sufficient frequency in the next few weeks to become obvious and ominous.

Poets and Reporters

While interpretative distortions were taking place at one level, factual distortions in the news itself were taking place at a different level. As a convenience to the media and as a way of keeping them supplied with accurate information, a press room was set up in police headquarters on the first day of the riot; most of the local and national news conferences in which Romney, Cavanagh, and Vance were involved were held in this special facility. Several dozen phone lines were provided for the press, and the constant flow of vital information collected from field command posts, bureaus, and other municipal departments was duplicated and passed along to the newsmen. Understandably, of course, many still went out on the streets into the riot areas. Despite the trouble this caused on the first day of the riot, newsmen were not forbidden in an area unless it was considered personally dangerous at particular times.

The lengths to which some newsmen went to get their stories, however, did not come to light until the inspector in charge of Kiefer command post unceremoniously directed a group of them off the grounds with orders they not be readmitted. The angry protest of an editor caused an inquiry into the matter, which in turn revealed reporters not only were pestering harried police command officers for details and background material for their stories, but also had developed the technique of stationing themselves where they could monitor police radio calls. Unfamiliar in many instances with the police code or with the fact that from one-third to two-thirds of the runs dispatched by radio were based on false reports, reporters were writing stories describing fierce gun battles that were not taking place, scores of bodies that never existed, and dozens of burning buildings that were never set on fire.

In a number of instances the riot reporting consequently turned out to be incredible distortions of what actually took place. During the week of the riot the *Detroit Free Press* somehow managed to work the phrase "Negro rioters" into the first sentence of most of its lead stories. The riot was four days old before local papers began to give any slight indication of looting and sniping by white persons. One radio station blanketed its affiliate stations on the east coast with a story that the riot had grown out of the fatal shooting of a Negro prostitute by two police vice squad officers—a rumor that was three weeks old in Detroit at the time of the riot and has not been substantiated yet.

A syndicated columnist of national renown flew to Detroit on the second night of the riot and in less than 24 hours was filing stories purporting to give the background of Detroit's racial trouble, writing how the mayor had been dealing with "handshaking black preachers instead of real leadership," and giving graphic portraits of how the blacks started the riot and how the whites were trying to quell it.

Was the Riot a Race Riot?

Negro Leadership

By far the most serious distortion in the press was the way it interpreted the role of Negro leadership in the city. A story by Jerome Aumente, the reporter who had written the penetrating series in the *Detroit News* on the urban crisis and had accompanied a team of Negroes trying to persuade the crowds to disperse peacefully on 12th street that Sunday morning, gave a factual, chronological account of their futile efforts. Aumente's story was matched, however, by a *Detroit Free Press* article entitled, "Could Quicker Action, or Stronger Action, Have Prevented It?" In part the article read:

> Of Negro leadership, it is fair to say there was none. The Negroes who enjoy the term leader—and thus gain access to such powers as Mayor Cavanagh, Girardin, the City Council, newspapers, the broadcasting media, the annual Negro banquets—were useless in this crisis.
>
> Many on-the-scene observers believe that no more than 100 (or perhaps 50) Negroes—teachers, local ministers, foremen in factories, mothers, storeowners, athletes—could have quelled the riot in its early stages by moving through the crowds, talking to residents, saying they were foolish, asking them to go home. It does not seem demanding to suggest such a task force should have been organized months ago—ready for mobilization at a moment's notice.

In the weeks that followed, this naive theme would become an often repeated one, partially encouraged by the same reporter, who became entranced with the brilliance of his own suggestion, and in a bolder mood would later write an article entitled, "How Negro Leadership Failed." The naiveté was not in the suggestion of a task force of community peace envoys. That strategy had occurred to both the Negro community and the police department years before and had been used with success in the Kercheval incident a year earlier. Actually, over 20 such persons were out in the 12th street area that July morning—local ministers, Negro union officials, block club and civil rights group leaders. The technique was tried—and it failed. What the press failed to understand was that this failure was no more an indictment of Negro leadership than the antics of Breakthrough, a local right-wing white organization, or the Mafia are indictments of white leadership. The clear implication of this accusation was that a (if not *the*) valid test of Negro leadership is whether or not it can stop Negroes from rioting—a theory that is as crass as it is unenlightened and misinformed. In spite of this, however, the failure-of-Negro-leadership philosophy became a popular interpretation whose full influence was not felt until after the riot was over.

There were also other ill-concealed and inept attempts to wrest a racial meaning from the riot. On the Tuesday of the riot a local television station quoted an unnamed Negro newsman as saying:

> Some people have tried to stick a racial tag on this thing. Responsible Negro people in the community won't buy that. This is nothing but pure lawlessness and it has nothing to do with race. Both black and white are taking part and not against each other. It was touched off by a minority of troublemakers and the people who don't or won't use their heads were sucked in.

Then in apparent oblivion to what it had just said, the editorial announced:

> If a mob of whites poured into any white business section, looted the stores and burned them, no one would call it a race riot, it would be called hooliganism or vandalism. And this in Detroit is exactly the same thing.

The intent of this comment was presumably a sincere attempt to warn white citizens against "sticking a racial tag" on the holocaust. Unfortunately, however, it gave the impression that there were no whites who were looting and burning, and thus a popular misconception was given further circulation.

Ironically, one of the most perceptive interpretations of the riot appeared in a chain of suburban newspapers published by Philip Power, an alert young journalist who at one time had served as administrative assistant to G. Mennen Williams. In his *Observer* newspapers, Power and his staff hammered at the theme that suburban residents could not run from the problems of Detroit's ghetto, nor could they shirk the responsibility of participating in the task of finding solutions to the racial and economic problems they had helped to create. The papers noted on August 2:

> There are both whites and Negroes among those arrested last week in looting. Both whites and Negroes were killed by snipers, and there are unconfirmed reports that white snipers were operating in Detroit last week. . . .
>
> Reports kept coming into this office on Monday and Tuesday of white teenagers seen smashing store windows as the looting moved out along Grand River. Police authorities have suggested that at least some of the people doing the looting out in this direction were not residents of the inner city . . . For a long time, some people in the suburbs have tried to argue that they and their communities are in some way separate from the inner city of Detroit. They aren't. In fact, the suburbs and the inner city are linked by the tightest sort of bonds . . . Involved? You bet. We're all involved in the worst riots since 1943. And if we don't do anything about it, we're likely to find that the riots of July 1967 weren't the last.

The National and International Press Pontificates

The role of the press in a free society has always been a much debated issue. Its reporting and interpreting of crisis situations have also been open to much criticism, long before riots began making the headlines. A major problem the press faces lies in this very area; it has the task not only of reporting facts but also of interpreting them, of writing what in one sense, at least, is instant history. In a crisis of the magnitude that Detroit faced, this difficult assignment was attempted not only by local newsmen, whose limited knowledge of race relations is notorious, but also by national and international journalists who flew into the city and did not even know where 12th street and police headquarters were, not to mention the complexity of the factors underlying what transpired.

Such a dilemma is compounded by the temptation to pontificate—not only to describe what but also to tell why. The very nature of the reporter's tasks in a riot situation demands of the journalistic profession an omniscience making it instantaneously and equally expert on military techniques, local and state politics, the economics of poverty, the history of race relations, problems of the urban ghetto, Negro leadership, and numerous other weighty issues. In some instances this awesome responsibility in the Detroit riot was assumed not only by newsmen and reporters, but by cameramen and photographers as well, whose subjective choice of the scenes they filmed or the people and situations they photographed became an integral part of the overall interpretation of the riot.

Accordingly, the reporting of the Detroit riot was marked not only by incredible distortions of the facts, but also by an even more serious distortion of the reasons behind the riot, although there were notable exceptions. And yet it is the mass media which mold and shape public opinion. They were the primary sources from which 98 percent of those who would hear about Detroit's disaster, and make some personal judgment about it, would get their information. Viewed against the quality of reporting during the 1943 riot, that of 1967 was a vast improvement. From the perspective of what actually happened, it left a great deal to be desired.

5. Riot Response: The Community

Community Leadership Fails to Prevail

Most of the city was literally asleep when the first signs of trouble began to develop on 12th street. The last of the Saturday night revelers were drifting home and their places on the streets were being taken by Sunday churchgoers, many on their way to early Mass. As the day passed, many Detroiters continued the Sunday pattern of going to the city's churches and parishes, unaware of the disorder that was steadily increasing on the near west side. Up until noon, for example, people continued to arrive at Grace Episcopal Church at 12th and Virginia Park, in the heart of the riot area, without realizing until they were within a few blocks of the church that it was in a sea of chaos. Those who stayed for services also did not realize that as morning prayers were recited in the sanctuary, a group of community leaders were huddled in the rector's office, mapping what would be a futile strategy to try to quell the disturbance by persuading the crowds to disperse.

The initial efforts of community leadership were concerned with the disorder itself and ways to stop it. When these efforts failed, community energies were directed toward some of the riot's effects rather than the riot itself. Of primary importance was the destruction of food supplies and shelter that residents of the riot areas were experiencing. By Monday grocery stores and markets which had escaped damage were being rapidly cleaned out by the concerned and the panic-striken who were anxious to have a sufficient supply of food "for the duration," however long that might be. Some merchants took advantage of the situation and drastically increased their prices. By Tuesday morning bread was selling in some stores in riot areas for 50¢ a loaf, and milk for 80¢ a half gallon. News of this exploitation reached the common council, which responded with a hastily drafted but no-nonsense ordinance banning such practices and setting a stiff penalty for violators. In spite of this the practice of scalping prices continued; before the week was over two violators had been arrested and taken to court.

Such distasteful examples of human response to a crisis situation were offset by the large volume of phone calls that began to pour into police headquarters and other city agencies as early as the first night of the riot. These calls were from both city and suburban residents offering their help to riot victims. Some offered their homes for displaced families, others offered to send food, clothing or money to assist in the large relief efforts that would develop. By Monday morning the Roman Catholic Archbishop's Committee on Human Relations had begun a massive canvass of suburban homes to find temporary lodging for riot victims. Under the aegis of the Detroit Council of Churches, Protestants launched an equally massive collection and distribution system of food and clothing.

The Interfaith Emergency Committee

Exemplary of the strong ecumenical spirit that characterizes Detroit religious communities, on Tuesday the efforts of the Catholics and Protestants were joined with the interests of the Jewish and Orthodox communities to form the Interfaith Emergency Committee, which operated one of the major riot relief programs both during and after the disaster.

The Interfaith Committee literally preempted the head-quarters of the Episcopal diocese of Michigan and set in motion a vast network of collection points for food and clothing throughout southeastern Michigan, with distribution outlets in churches throughout the riot area. Tons of food and clothing were made available to its victims during the riot's first week. The scene at the diocesan building was, in its own way, as impressive and as dramatic as that at police headquarters. Episcopal Bishop Richard Emrich, who was at his summer farm in Vermont when news of the riot reached him, drove all night back to Detroit and reached his office only to find it had become the nerve center of the relief operation. The bishop is reported to have quietly retreated to his secretary's office where he began to assist in the relief work.

One of the major tasks of the Interfaith Committee was the creation of an emergency chaplaincy service to the thousands of persons in custody. By 4 p.m. Saturday, July 29, over 70 Detroit area clergymen were being dispatched in teams of two to work four-hour shifts around the clock in the police precincts, the county jail, and the temporary detention facility on Belle Isle. The emergency chaplains had emerged in response to two growing tension points in the community. The first was the widespread anxiety of many Detroiters whose missing relatives were presumed to be in custody. Of equal concern, however, were the proliferating stories of the mistreatment of prisoners that had begun to circulate about mid-week during the riot. The Interfaith Committee petitioned Girardin for permission to enter the police precinct and detention facilities to establish what the Reverend Charles Butler, a leading Negro cleric, termed a "ministry of presence," hoping thereby not only to offer assistance to prisoners but also, simply by being on the scene, to dissuade improper handling of prisoners by policemen and guardsmen. Careful guidelines for this operation were worked out between the clergy and Girardin's staff, and were distributed to each clergyman along with a written pass requesting police officials to "provide access after curfew hours to prisoner-custodial facilities." Once the program was inaugurated, the chaplains were able to make contacts for prisoners with their families or employers, to assist in the transfer of ill prisoners from jail facilities to hospitals, and in some cases to effect the release of prisoners whose arrests had resulted from understandable but regrettable mistakes. When the operation was concluded the week following the riot, police officials, who had initially looked upon the chaplains somewhat less than enthusiastically, were almost unanimous in their praise for the assistance they had rendered, and Girardin expressed his personal regret that the service had not been inaugurated earlier during the riot week.

The Civil Rights Commission

Stories of the mistreatment of prisoners had also come to the attention of the state Civil Rights Commission. On July 28 the commission dispatched telegrams to President Johnson, Romney, Cavanagh, Vance, other state and local law enforcement officials, and state and local bar associations urging

> that due process be instituted immediately for all prisoners held in our jails for charges related to the riots; that fair bond be set; that those held for minor offenses be released on personal bond; that every precaution be taken to prevent any action that may be regarded as police brutality . . . that equal protection of the law be assured for all persons; that judges be sent to out-state locations where persons are being held so that arraignments may be immediately instituted; that illegal search and seizures be stopped . . . To this end the Commission requests authority to station staff observers in all police precincts and places of detention of prisoners.

The request for staff observers in police precincts and jail facilities was a clear indication that the charges of police brutality were of the gravest concern to the commission. Girardin accepted the request and made arrangements for commission staff personnel to be admitted along with the Interfaith Committee chaplains.

The presence of these non-police personnel, once their purpose was made clear to precinct officials, undoubtedly had a calming effect on police operations, which by this time were beginning to show the effects of prolonged pressure and fatigue. In some instances, however, this combination of police and non-police personnel in the precincts gave rise to situations which became classic examples of the difference between appearance and reality in many riot cases. Commission observers, for example, had no sooner arrived at the first precinct station on Saturday afternoon than they witnessed two officers carry a prisoner by stretcher to a patrol wagon, apparently for conveyance to the city hospital a block away. The prisoner's head was a mass of blood and bruises. It was somewhat understandable, therefore, that the observers concluded they had arrived just in time to see the aftermath of a vicious case of police brutality. They were not alone in their assumption. John Doar, assistant U.S. attorney general who was in Detroit for most of the riot week, happened to be passing through and also witnessed the scene. He lost no time in bringing the case to Girardin's attention, who immediately requested a full report on the situation. As it turned out from the eye-witness reports of fellow inmates, confinement had apparently been too much an emotional strain for the prisoner; his bruises were the self-inflicted result of banging his head against the prison cell bars. Further investigation indicated that he had incurred head wounds a day earlier in an unsuccessful attempt to leap through the window of a police bus and was forcibly restrained by other prisoners. One potential police brutality statistic quickly evaporated.

Police Fatigue and the Looters

The legal profession in the city also lost no time in tackling the immense problems developing from the necessity of recovering the vast amounts of loot taken during the riot. A day after the disorder broke, police headquarters had become flooded with anonymous tips on the locations of stolen goods. Some tips came from irate neighbors who had watched in horror as "the family next door" or "across the street" unloaded vans or car trunks filled with furniture, clothing, or appliances. Other tips came from vindictive persons who saw a unique opportunity to embarrass or "get even with" a neighbor merely by enticing the police into making a thorough house search. In a number of instances, especially as word passed through the community that police were beginning to recover loot, calls came from looters themselves. Apparently suffering conscience pangs or fearful their premises might be searched, they called the police to report discovering, say, six color television sets in their bedroom or three toasters in their kitchen. The callers were always at a loss to know how the loot got there but were equally insistent that the culprit who had played such a malicious trick on them be promptly apprehended and brought to justice!

In the first few days of the riot the police actually had little time to track down and recover loot; their main concern was quelling the disorder on the streets. Tips were assigned to appropriate precincts, however, and scout cars were dispatched to effect some recoveries, mainly during daylight hours. As could be anticipated, this arrangement was pregnant with problems. In some instances bewildered police officers, acting legitimately but on false tips, entered homes to confront surprised and incensed householders, protesting their brand new television sets had been purchased a week earlier. In most cases the confusion was resolved by confiscating the articles in dispute. In other cases police officers, whose academy training in courtesy and good human relations was already wearing dangerously thin, simply asked no questions and listened to no explanations, but took whatever seemed suspect.

The Lawyers

The initial response to this dilemma came from police executives themselves. Acting upon a growing number of complaints, Girardin organized a special squad of detectives to give full attention to the recovery of loot. These officers developed the technique of going to homes or places of business identified in tips and requesting the permission of residents to search the premises. They reported that even in cases where loot was recovered, they were not refused permission to enter.

The volume of stolen goods and the number of complaints dictated a recovery operation more extensive than could be conducted by a small squad of men. It was at this juncture that the legal profession entered, led by the Neighborhood Legal Services Center. The center filed suit in circuit court requesting an injunction against "illegal searches and seizures." The suit was subsequently dismissed, but it led to the acceptance of a compromise plan, hammered out between NLSC, the Wayne County prosecutor, and police officials. The joint agreement called for searches to be conducted only after securing the signed permission of householders on a form prepared by the prosecutor's office. Even operating under these strict regulations, sufficient loot was recovered to fill the police gymnasium and a large part of the city's main transportation garage. This awe-inspiring mountain of recovered property, including everything from pencils and rifles to refrigerators, was estimated to be only one-fourth of the goods stolen during the riot.

The Community Assessment

It was inevitable that the community response should entail a great many public statements about the making and meaning of the riot. Some were romanticized nonsense, written and spoken by people who felt an unexplainable need to consecrate the violence and translate it into the litany of a holy crusade. One national study termed the central problem of the riots to be one of communication. "Angry, desperate people do not communicate their feelings to anyone else because they are not asked," an article in the *Christian Century* of August 23, 1967, quoted the study as declaring. "Convinced that no one will listen to their complaints, that city administrators do not care about their

9. National guardsmen and federal troops at Kercheval and Van Dyke, on the city's east side. At no time during the riot were federal troops deployed west of Woodward avenue, the area of the city that suffered the greatest damage.

10. Embattled firemen and policemen on 12th street. The fire truck shows signs of damage from sniper fire while the shoe in the foreground apparently represents loot dropped earlier in the day by someone in haste.

11. "Mission Impossible," hastily scrawled on the side of this U.S. army tank, summed up the feeling not only of law enforcement personnel, but of many Detroiters as well. This intersection is directly west of the Harlan House Motel, where 50-year-old Helen Hall was fatally shot by a stray bullet.

12. The women's bath house on Belle Isle, Detroit's principal recreation park in the Detroit River. Dubbed "Belcatraz" by its inmates, it was one of the major but makeshift detention facilities for persons arrested during the riot.

problems, they decide that the only recourse left them is violence and rioting."

Such assessments attributed a rationalization by rioters about why they rioted that interviews with arrested rioters in Detroit did not confirm. In an overwhelming number of instances rioters in Detroit had no clear-cut notion of why they broke windows or looted or both. "It was something to do," or "Everyone else was doing it," they said. These national analyses also showed an appalling insensitivity to the proclamations on both the national and local scene of the black nationalists, who were at least quite honest and explicit about what they were doing, why they were doing it, and what they deemed was at stake—and it was not the desire for better communication with city hall. The "despair theory" and the "consecration-of-violence" interpretations also became increasingly obnoxious to many Negroes who lived where the violence was taking place, rather than in the security of academia or suburbia where many riot analyses were written. For Negroes in the ghetto, the anatomy of the riot was the analysis and assessment of a nightmare, and they were exceptionally unsympathetic to scholarly, political, or publicist attempts to interpret it otherwise.

One of the more sensitive local assessments was issued on July 28 by Bishop Emrich, chairman of the Citizens Committee for Equal Opportunity. In a declaration that summed up the sentiments of many Negro and white Detroiters, he wrote:

Because it is important how we react to tragedy, and because thought influences action, the Citizens Committee has asked me as its chairman to make this statement.

First, it is important that we maintain confidence in our city, and that we do not waste time picking political scape-goats or hurling abuse at one another. Let reaction be constructive and practical.

For the good of Detroit we must point out that this was not a racial riot. The looting and sniping were integrated. The major part of the riot was a criminal attack upon property, which stunned the great majority of people, both white and Negro, and which must be punished. But there was no racial warfare, which means that we can assume the basic unity of the city and look forward to rebuilding and working together.

Second, we can learn together the vicious character of extremism, white or Negro; for it seems probable that advocates of such extreme and divisive positions were responsible for the sniping. This extreme thought is disastrous, suicidal, and criminal; and together we can spew it out in the name of sanity. People who hate become hate-full people. The thought of this small minority must be declared to be out of bounds in the name of civilization. If we learn that, we will have learned a lesson that can bless us. It is men of good will who are "Soul Brothers," whatever their race.

Third, why did Negro mobs jeer Negro leaders who sought to restrain them? The answer can be understood under the heading of private property. Those of us, Negro and white, who own property, have a stake in America and want order for obvious reasons. But suppose that people own no property, have no such obvious stake in America, and feel alienated from the blessings of a great country. Why should they fear anarchy? What have they, who have nothing, got to lose?

This is a great continuing problem. We must build an America in which every man has an obvious stake, property, and hope. We urge Federal government, and specifically Congress, to enact legislation which can help us to deal with these basic causes of civic unrest. And the private sector in all of its institutions, and everyman, has a contribution to make. If we react properly, Detroit can rise a better city. The only rational goal is one America, united and working together.

And, in closing, the gratitude of us all to the police, firemen, and troops, to the public servants, and volunteer people of good will who have been a credit to the city in a grim time.

H. Rap Brown's Visit

Exactly one month after the disorder occurred, Detroit was host to H. Rap Brown, national chairman of the Student Non-Violent Coordinating Committee. His appearance under the auspices of the *Inner City Voice*, a recently founded publication of young black nationalists in Detroit, was scheduled for Sunday afternoon, August 27. It is both fair and accurate to say that no speaker in Detroit ever received a greater advanced build-up than Brown. The local press, radio, and television carried reports of his impending visit for days prior to his arrival, as did national network news programs. One Negro Detroiter observed, "If General Motors had wanted to spend five million dollars on promoting a new automobile, they could not have received as much advance publicity as did Rap's visit."

Such extensive publicity created a considerable amount of tension and anxiety in the city among both Negroes and whites, who feared a fresh outbreak of violence. Few realized that Brown has seldom if ever managed to be on the scene when actual large-scale riots have erupted. Nevertheless, the police department prepared for any eventuality; a sizable number of patrolmen were assigned to the 10th precinct station, less than half a mile from the Dexter Theatre, where Brown was to speak. Several anonymous phone callers threatened to assassinate Brown while he was in the city, and although his colleagues refused an offer of police escort, the problem of protecting him was placed in the highly capable hands of Inspector James Bannon, head of the criminal intelligence bureau. Bannon and his staff spent the afternoon in a security operation that would have taxed the patience and endurance of the entire force of a small town police department. Finally, a minimum number of officers were placed on traffic duty in the area around the theatre. Department executives assembled at the precinct station to await the outcome.

As it happened, the biggest problem of the afternoon was traffic. Less than 2,000 people turned out to hear Brown, but on a commercial thoroughfare surrounded by a residential community with no parking available, that many created one enormous traffic jam. A large number of motorists also cruised the area. Whether they were potential attenders at the rally, or simply the curious who did not want to leave the assumed safety of their cars, is not known. In any case, they contributed to traffic congestion in the area.

There was one incident during the afternoon that shed considerable light on several facets of the problem of racial tension. Because the theatre's capacity was less than 1,000, about half the people who came to hear Brown stood outside during the rally. The congestion and volume of traffic drew a large number of on-lookers and youngsters, apparently attracted by the crowd. There was also the usual large complement of radio, television, and press trucks, camera crews and personnel in the area, which added to the excitement. As the rally was winding up, some youngsters outside the theatre began to taunt one of the camera crews. Someone threw a bottle at a cameraman who, in a move that defied both logic and sanity, picked up the bottle and flung it back into the crowd. For a few moments there was real trouble. Part of the crowd descended on the cameraman and his cohorts, demolishing a press car and wrecking camera equipment. Another portion of the crowd—as on the Sunday morning of a month earlier, they consisted mainly of young men—proceeded down Dexter avenue breaking windows. The police were on top of the situation almost immediately, and though one officer was injured by flying glass, the incident was over almost as quickly as it had started.

The press as a whole was strangely silent about the incident and what triggered it. One radio-television station a week later took the police to task for not giving the press better protection! The WXYZ editorial read in part:

> Nothing Brown had to say in Detroit surprised WXYZ. He simply repeated comments we've heard many times before.
>
> However, we are concerned that Detroit officials still are not willing to accept the idea that Brown's statements, or the activities of his followers, really are a threat to law and order in our community. Newsmen were injured as they tried to fulfill their responsibility to keep the public informed. An unmarked police car parked a block away was stoned . . . and a policeman injured . . . As has been the case in far too many instances in recent months, the police protection for the citizens of Detroit that is so urgently needed in these perilous times was missing. It's fortunate that only some minor injuries were the result.

Like so much of the community, WXYZ is angered by this apparent unwillingness or inability of Detroit law enforcement officials to protect our citizens from mob violence. It makes us question how far responsible Detroiters will have to be pushed before they are again given assurance that the law is also there to protect them.

Reports from observers at the scene strongly suggest that it may have been a WXYZ cameraman whose ineptitude started the fracas. For many who did know the facts behind this event, it became a graphic example of the less creditable ways in which the mass media can become actively involved in potentially explosive situations.

Public and Private Social Agencies

The response to the riot by public and private social agencies was one of the high points of the riot and post-riot period. Generally it was upon these agencies that the bulk of the relief work fell, along with the task of helping the city to return to some degree of normalcy. Under the constant prodding of the mayor's office, the public works and sanitation departments dealt with the physical scars of the riot in a highly efficient manner. By four months after the riot, many of the damaged buildings had been razed and the ground leveled.

But the enormous social scars presented a far different picture. By the fifth day of the riot, for example, over 400 families had been registered by agencies of the United Community Services. These families had become separated during the previous five days and were seeking help in locating missing members. In addition, over 700 phone calls flooded UCS switchboards in a two-day period from persons trying to locate a spouse or some other member of the family. Employers also enlisted the aid of UCS in their frantic searches for missing delivery trucks and drivers. Apparently, in the confusion of the first few days, drivers legitimately engaged in trucking goods from wholesale to retail outlets either had been apprehended as suspected looters or had taken advantage of the chaotic situation to haul their cargoes out of town.

United Community Services, together with the Mayor's Development Team created immediately after the riot, eventually became the primary clearing house agencies for long-term housing relocation, food, and clothing needs. One of the most ambitious private programs was organized by Dr. Sally W. Cassidy, a Wayne State University professor and a leading Roman Catholic laywoman. Called "Homes By Christmas," the group set as its goal the relocation of as many families as possible who lost their homes during the disorder. Homes By Christmas conducted its relocation campaign in both city and suburban communities, raised almost $150,000, and directly assisted in the permanent settlement of more than a hundred families.

The development team directed its attention toward a major analysis and restructuring of municipal agencies in order to provide more effective and efficient city services to the community. The mayor had contemplated such an undertaking months before the riot, which simply made it more imperative. Led by Richard Strichartz, former city controller who had returned to his post as general counsel at Wayne State University, the team coopted on a loan basis key social welfare experts from agencies throughout the city, including Harold Johnson, associate director of the Neighborhood Services Organization and lecturer in the School of Social Work at the University of Michigan, and Dave Casson of the Merrill-Palmer Institute's faculty and subsequently head of Detroit's model cities program. Nearly everyone in the city recognized that Detroit could not be rebuilt, neither physically nor socially, to what it had been before the riot. However, there was ample activity to give the city hope that a new Detroit could be created.

Rebuilding the City

On Thursday of the riot week Vance, Romney, and Cavanagh called a mass meeting of community leaders to discuss the task of rebuilding the city. The aides of all three men worked on the meeting for a full day, coordinating agenda items, lists of speakers and persons to be invited, and a myriad of additional details. The meeting itself was something of a political miracle, representing as it did the interests of the Democratic mayor, the Republican governor, and the envoy of the White House. Three days earlier this triumvirate had had notable differences about how to deal with the riot itself. When it finally convened, the whole spectrum of positions, thoughts, and opinions in Detroit was represented, from the city's most conservative business and political interests to the most outspoken of the militants. It had been noted that the governor of New Jersey and the mayor of Newark had emerged from their disaster with the hope that it would provide a basis for dialogue between blacks and whites. No such problem existed in Detroit; there was, however, the problem of moving from rhetoric to action.

The New Detroit Committee

Detroit's answer was the New Detroit Committee, a joint enterprise of Cavanagh and Romney. Together they agreed for chairman on 35-year-old Joseph L. Hudson Jr., scion of one of the city's oldest and best-known families, and head of Detroit's largest department store. The New Detroit Committee membership was a combination of traditional committee names, both black and white, along with some new faces representing community groups and militant organizations. Less than 20 percent of its membership was black, and it failed to include representatives of small Negro businesses. But even with these flaws, it was one of the most representative community efforts ever undertaken in Detroit.

At the outset the New Detroit Committee plunged into its assignment with determination. It managed to persuade the common council to declare a moratorium on building permits for damaged structures in the riot areas, a move designed to make sure that redevelopment plans would be created with residents of the affected communities as active participants. It also prevented many merchants with exploitative reputations, whose stores had been destroyed, from rebuilding and simultaneously recreating afresh explosive problems in the ghetto. The committee also launched, under the co-chairmanship of Stanley Winkelman, businessman and active community leader, and Dr. William R. Keast, president of Wayne State University, a series of hearings concerning law enforcement problems, which led to the sponsorship of an ill-fated study of police problems in Detroit by Arthur Brandstetter, director of the School of Police Science and Public Safety at Michigan State University.

Open Housing Legislation

For some reason the New Detroit Committee placed top priority on achieving the passage of open housing legislation at state and municipal levels. Considering the emotional fervor this issue creates in the white community among both liberals and bigots alike, and the tragic history of open housing legislation in Detroit, it is not surprising that New Detroit should have concluded that this battle was the key to breaking down barriers in Negro-white relationships. To many Negroes, however, the battle was an exercise in futility. They argued that open housing was a traditional white response to Negro demands, and that the proposed legislation was useless to low-income Negroes, those presumably involved in the riot, whose need was not for housing opportunities in suburbs, but for decent low-cost housing in the city. They further argued that even if the legislation passed, it would only represent a moral victory for white liberals and would have little effect on actual patterns of real estate transactions between Negroes and whites. In essence, it was argued, open housing legislation is a sham; it gives white people who work for its passage a feeling of doing something valuable and important for Negroes, when its actual impact is less than negligible.

In spite of this considerably cool reception that open housing received from the Negro masses, the New Detroit Committee made every conceivable effort to effect its passage in Detroit and in the state legislature. Its determination to secure a victory on the issue was symbolized by a massive lobbying effort in Lansing, the state capital, in which the giants of the automobile industry —Henry Ford II, James Roche, and Lynn Townsend—along with Hudson and other key Detroit civic figures personally attempted to persuade state legislators to vote for open housing. Eventually their efforts were successful, but the Detroit victory was a hollow one.

The Detroit open housing ordinance passed by a narrow margin in the city council and became the immediate target of a petition campaign led by some of the city's more active bigots, encouraged by Councilwoman Mary Beck. They had no difficulty in collecting sufficient signatures to force suspension of the ordinance's taking effect, and to require that it be put to the voters in the fall 1968 municipal elections. The city's liberals thus faced the prospect of raising money and expending vast amounts of energy and effort trying to salvage a legislative symbol the Detroit electorate had never approved, and even if approved, would be for all practical purposes meaningless.*

New Employment Opportunities

Beyond this debacle, however, important and positive actions are taking place in Detroit. Many of them are to the credit of the New Detroit Committee, others undoubtedly reflect the impact of thinking and discussion in New Detroit on its members and their constituencies. One of the most important areas where breakthroughs have been made is employment. Artificial testing practices have been dropped, experimental programs in hiring men previously labeled as functionally unemployable have been instituted, and some men with prison records are now finding

---

*A federal court ruling temporarily saved the ordinance from being placed on the ballot, on the grounds that a referendum would violate the equal protection clauses of the U.S. Constitution.

employment opportunities where they did not exist before. It is here that there was some concensus between Negroes and whites in the city. If a man has good, steady employment, he himself can handle the problems of self-dignity and self-determination, as well as the more immediate necessities of providing for his family, education for his children, and luxuries for himself. Whatever else the community felt, for the most part there was unanimity on the expansion of the job market for Negroes as one of the most important developments of the post-riot period.

II
An Interpretation of the Event

6. Riot Aftermath: New Dimensions of the Racial Struggle

Post-Bellum Negro Leadership

There are many people who insist that the rebellion in Detroit did not begin on July 23. It began, instead, in the early days of August, after the riot itself had been quelled. The rebellion was marked by an upheaval in power positions within the Negro community and in power relationships between blacks and whites in the city. In many ways the outcome of this power struggle is viewed by both black and white Detroiters as infinitely more important than the quelling of the riot.

One of the ironies of Detroit Negro history is that it has produced powerful spokesmen and cadres of disciples for every conceivable shade of racial philosophy. On one hand, the city has shaped the careers of such nationally-known scholar-statesmen as United Nations Under-Secretary Ralph Bunche and United States Appeals Court Judge Wade H. McCree. For years Detroit boasted the largest branch membership in the NAACP of any city in the nation. There are more members of the black bourgeoisie in Detroit—middle-class Negro property owners—than in any metropolitan area in the nation. This segment of the black populace has been the principal advocate of a bi-racial integrated society.

On the other hand, for decades Detroit has also had a small but brilliant and articulate group of proponents of various schools of black nationalism. In addition to being the birthplace of the Black Muslim movement, Detroit has spawned local chapters of the Revolutionary Action movement and the Freedom Now Party, together with such indigenous movements as the Group on Advanced Leadership. Their common tie has been a marked hostility to integrationist efforts; their leadership has been outspoken in denouncing any attempt to achieve racial progress that is predicated on the good will or sincerity of white Americans. These different groups have drawn varying responses from the city's Negro masses. Of those affiliated with any racial movement, by far the largest number has given token or active support to traditional integration-oriented organizations. At the same time the black nationalist movement has been moderately well-known; its pamphlets and papers receive wide circulation in the Negro community, and its spokesmen have been the subject of discussion and debate among Negroes for years.

Significantly, however, this wide spectrum of thought and philosophy in the Negro community has been little known among whites. The common assumption in the white community appears to have bordered on the belief that at birth every Negro receives a life-time membership in the NAACP, which in turn speaks ex-cathedra for all Negroes. As a matter of fact, if the handful of top Detroit decision-makers who became so dramatically interested and involved in the city's racial problems after the riot had listened to the NAACP and its counterparts in the months and years before July 23, 1967, the city might have been spared the destruction it experienced. Oddly enough, there was nothing the black nationalists said in the post-riot period about the frustration of being black in a white man's world, that NAACP leaders and others had not been saying for decades. With few exceptions, however, the white leadership in the city, led by business and industry spokemen, took the position that the traditional "moderate leadership" had been repudiated by the riot, that white spokesmen had been dealing with the wrong Negroes, and that they must now establish rapport with the new black leadership.

The way in which the new black leadership was identified became one of the more interesting aspects of post-riot Detroit. During the week of the riot itself there was only one public attempt to give the violence any strategic significance. Three days after the disorder erupted, two well-known spokesmen among the black nationalists, Milton and Richard Henry, sent telegrams to the White House, Governor Romney, and Mayor Cavanagh, which read:

> Regarding the insurrection in Detroit and speaking for the Malcolm X Society, we will ask for a cessation of all hostilities by insurrectionists by 7 p.m. today [Tuesday, July 25] provided the following eight points are accepted and are the basis of discussion by 1 p.m. today:
>
> 1. Withdraw all troops
> 2. Release all prisoners
> 3. Give amnesty to all insurrectionists
> 4. Establish district police commissioners
> 5. Agree to urban renewal veto by residents
> 6. Divide City Council and the school board by districts
> 7. Provide funds for community-owned businesses and co-operatives, allowing groups of Negroes to go into business for themselves
> 8. Institute compensatory and compulsory equal employment opportunity.

Curiously, the Henrys denied having any control over the insurrectionists, but suggested simultaneously that if they called for it, an end to the rioting would probably take place. Both Milton and Richard Henry were known to be men of considerable influence in the black nationalist community. Richard Henry had served at one time as president of the Group on Advanced Leadership and was a frequent writer for black nationalist publications. Milton Henry, an attorney and former councilman of Pontiac, a small municipality 20 miles north of Detroit and the site of a large General Motors plant, had also been a candidate for public office on the Freedom Now party ticket and enjoyed the reputation of being one of the most effective and articulate legal minds in the Negro community. Their bid to negotiate a settlement of the disorder was rejected, almost without comment, by the mayor and the governor. It was the first and last time the Henrys were heard from in an official capacity concerning the Detroit riot. The mantle of spokesman for the black nationalists passed to the equally well-known and eloquent 56-year-old Reverend Albert Cleage Jr., pastor of Detroit's Central United Church of Christ.

The Reverend Albert Cleage Jr.

To understand Albert Cleage is to gain a considerable measure of insight into the black nationalist community in America. He is a member of one of Detroit's oldest middle-class Negro families; his father was a Detroit physician, and his three brothers are also Detroiters. One is a physician, one owns a printing company, and the third is an attorney. The Cleage family were prominent members of Plymouth Congregational Church, a citadel of the black bourgeoisie in Detroit, whose present pastor the Reverend Nicholas Hood is also a city councilman. For several decades its spiritual leader was the Reverend Horace A. White, who developed a pulpit that has traditionally been a source of immense political influence in the city. Cleage grew up in Plymouth Congregational during White's pastorate, along with the brilliant University of Chicago theologian Dr. Nathan Scott. That a prominent church in the midst of one of the nation's most affluent black communities could produce two clergymen of such widely divergent philosophies is both ironic and symbolic of the deep-seated emotions white society has created in black America.

Cleage's own pastorate at Central United Church has an ironic quality all its own. A powerful orator, Cleage possesses that mysterious and charismatic quality of religious leadership that has often marked the careers of Negro clergymen, one that has given rise to such diverse figures as Nat Turner and Martin Luther King. Initially, Cleage was able to unify under his leadership a number of the segments of black nationalism in Detroit— an achievement noticeably lacking among black nationalists elsewhere in the United States. What this unity represented in terms of numbers is unknown and to a great extent unimportant. Men like Cleage have made black nationalism a force to be reckoned with in America's racial struggle.

Those who do not take solace in numbers, however, point to the fact that Cleage had never commanded any significant loyalty among Detroit's Negroes whenever his leadership was put to the test at the ballot box. An almost perennial candidate for public office in the past decade, Cleage successively lost in bids for governor, city councilman, and a seat on the board of education. His critics therefore insisted that it would take a municipal election to give a realistic appraisal of the strength of his position and following in the black community.

In the interim, and because of his post-riot rhetoric and its impact on segments of the white community, Cleage emerged as the most discussed and debated figure in Detroit's Negro community. On August 9, about a week after the riot ended, a mass meeting of the more militant black citizens was called in the City-County Building auditorium, the scene of the meeting convened by Vance, Romney, and Cavanagh a week earlier. Ostensibly the later meeting was to voice disapproval of the black representation on the New Detroit Committee, but it ended in the repudiation of the committee itself and the creation of an all-black organization. A recommendation that the New Detroit Committee's membership be half Negro was verbally rejected by Cleage and Milton Henry. This recommendation, which would have committed the militants to a bi-racial effort in rebuilding the city, never was put to a vote. Instead, James Del Rio, state representative, proposed that the New Detroit Committee be made advisory to the organization about to be formed by the militants, with the militants making the decisions. This proposal passed, and shortly thereafter the City-wide Citizens Action Committee was formed, with Cleage as its chairman.

From this new position of strength, Cleage began his assault on the white establishment. For reasons peculiar to the current climate of racial attitudes in the white community, he found ready and willing allies among the whites. Cleage's first approach was to the Interfaith Emergency Committee, which had over $80,000 in undisbursed funds, remaining from contributions by churches and individuals for the relief of riot victims. Although the Interfaith Committee enjoyed wide ecumenical support, its most active white leaders were predominantly young clerics, many of whom were new to the city and were outspoken critics of the establishment in both white and Negro Detroit churches. For several years prior to the riot many of these young clerics had been engaged in heated controversy with their older and more conservative colleagues on a number of inner-city issues, including religious support for Detroit's Alinsky-based West Central Organization. On this latter issue the white militants had received less than enthusiastic support from the Negro clergy, causing them to dismiss the majority of Negro clerics as misguided tools of the white establishment or proverbial Uncle Toms or both. The sudden wealth of the Interfaith Committee gave the young clerics both the resources and the structure they had previously lacked to support militant causes. Accordingly, when Cleage requested funds from the interfaith group for the first of many projects he would put forth, he received a grant of $19,500, over the strenuous objections of a small but vocal minority.

Cleage's influence with members of the New Detroit Committee was far greater and far more significant. Initially, Cleage's group had taken the position that the New Detroit Committee, with its bi-racial establishment-oriented membership, should be advisory to black-sponsored rebuilding efforts. When this did not materialize, several representatives of the militant group who had been invited to join and had accepted membership on the New Detroit Committee found themselves drummed out of the militants' ranks. It was not long, however, before a series of closed-door meetings between Cleage and the captains of Detroit industry began to receive widespread, and in the minds of many, well-planned publicity. National publications carried stories of Henry Ford II's making a pilgrimage to Cleage's church in the heart of the riot area for a lengthy meeting, with top aides of both men present. Joseph L. Hudson Jr., chairman of the New Detroit Committee, made repeated public statements after private meetings with Cleage that led the community to anticipate that a truce, if not a potential working agreement, was in the making.

The Federation for Self-Determination

That more than a truce was in the offing became evident as Cleage began to submit a series of requests for funds to the New Detroit Committee. When committee members initially balked at a requested $137,000 grant, Hudson and Ford personally pledged to raise 25 percent of the funds. A larger request of $750,000 from the Ford Foundation gained the personal endorsement of many New Detroit Committee members. Sizable grants to a second Cleage-initiated organization, the Federation for Self-Determination, began to flow in from organizations outside Detroit, including some $80,000 from national religious bodies.

This dramatic and tangible turn of events drew mixed reactions in the Negro community, most of which, however, remained private and personal grumblings of discontent. On the one hand, many Negroes were amazed by the willingness of the white community to respond so generously to Cleage's demands, mixed with veiled public suggestions that if they were not met, the city could expect bigger and bolder trouble. At the same time, however, these Negroes meticulously avoided open criticism of Cleage. Their commitment to the racial struggle and the plight of the city's black populace forced them to the tacit admission that if Cleage could deliver, if he could get action from white institutions and leaders whose prior involvement had been minimal or peripheral, then the end result would justify the new strategy. Simultaneously, they shook their heads and muttered in despair at that new strategy, and what they took to be an affirmation of its validity, by the way in which white leadership supported black militancy.

The White Business Establishment

Torn between racial loyalties on one hand, and the apparent scuttling of the philosophy of non-violent change not only by blacks but even by decision-making whites on the other, the bulk of Detroit's Negro leaders turned their anger toward the white business establishment. They saw little separating their militant articulation of the racial problem and that of the nationalists led by Cleage. But they also saw the white business community give the nationalist position a new credence, and from their perspective, an unwarranted status by the massive infusion of white money and personal involvement. It was a development the traditional Negro leadership dared not criticize, on the assumption that even money in the hands of militant nationalists might somehow get translated into low-cost housing, the development of a stable political organization, or job-training programs. However, because the traditional sectors of black leadership had always contended for these same goals, they began to interpret the actions of the whites as a crude and not-too-subtle form of buying protection from the nationalists. The off-the-record comments of white leadership did not help to disabuse this theory. Several white businessmen were widely quoted throughout the Negro community as having said privately that since traditional black leadership had not been able to stop the riots, they would have to deal with someone who could. To many Negroes the crassness of this philosophy was only exceeded by its ignorance.

Thus, three months after the riot a struggle for political power and leadership of immense proportions was taking place in black Detroit. For most Negroes who cared one way or the other, it was a battle of black people about black people, and by black

people, from which white influence and power should have been
noticeably absent. Although they were seeking large amounts of
white money, the nationalists were committed to the exclusion
of white influence by the concept of self-determination. This in-
congruity was not lost upon many in the traditional leadership
camp. The traditionalists, on the other hand, were firmly convinced that if white influence were not injected into the struggle,
the mass of black people in Detroit would ultimately determine
which philosophy would prevail. They were equally certain that
middle-class aspirations and attainments would win out, and
that violence as a strategy for change would be repudiated.

The Detroit Council of Organizations

In the early phase of the struggle the traditionalist sentiment
had crystallized into the formation of the Detroit Council of
Organizations led by the Reverend Roy A. Allen, another of the
city's noted Negro pastors. The council's list of supporting organizations comprised an impressive array of Negro organizations,
including the Negro Ministers Alliance, the Urban League, the
Cotillion Club, the local chapter of CORE, congressional district
organizations, block club associations, and union groups. Its
existence was made precarious by the fact that several member
organizations brought ancient internecine hostilities with them
into the council, and by the difficulty its leaders had of even
gaining an audience with white business leadership. The Council of Organizations had the numbers, and if a count had been
taken, they would have had the mass of Negro support in the
city. The City-wide Citizens Action Committee had the money
and the influence in the white sector. Between the two groups
all the facets of a political revolution could be seen. The old
guard apparently had been toppled, a new regime enthroned,
and life for the masses went on as usual.

Many saw in the lack of tangible progress in the physical rebuilding of the city or of substantive changes in the critical areas
of education, employment, and law enforcement, the basic fail-

ure of all three groups New Detroit, Council of Organizations, and Citizens Action Committee. What had transpired thus far had been a series of exercises in rhetoric, a jockeying for power positions, an interesting shift of ideologies; but there had been little visible effect on the lives of the black masses.

"Message to the Black Nation"

The next stage in the struggle within the Negro community saw a new political maturity rise to the fore. Ironically, it was the formation of the Federation for Self-Determination which brought it about. Early in December 1967 Cleage attempted to bring all the groups in the black community under one superstructure. In one of his less brilliant strategic moves, Cleage had himself named chairman. In spite of efforts to convince him that a person less identified with either camp would be needed at the helm to achieve an effective federation, Cleage insisted on being chairman.

Under ordinary circumstances this would have been an extremely propitious time for a test of strength. It became such when the announcement of the Federation carried the Detroit Council of Organizations as one of its member groups. Renouncing a pact the Cleage and Allen forces had made not to publicly criticize each others' operations, Allen released a statement condemning both the Federation and its white financial supporters. Cleage responded in kind by labeling Allen and his cohorts "tools of Cavanagh and Walter Reuther." The battle was joined and Negro leaders who had been trying diligently to avoid over-identification with either group found themselves forced to choose sides.

This confrontation resulted in defections from the ranks of the Council of Organizations and the beginning of strange alliances with the Federation. Several groups which had initially renounced Cleage's efforts and aligned themselves with the Council of Organizations found their top leadership moving silently to Cleage's Federation camp. Louis Simmons, president of the powerful

Wolverine Bar Association, and James Garret, president of the bourgeois-oriented Cotillion Club, were among the first to transfer allegiance from the Council to the Federation. Others who had remained aloof from the organizational struggle began to affiliate with Cleage's efforts. Such stalwarts of Negro leadership as Longworth Quinn, editor of the *Michigan Chronicle*, August Calloway, chairman of the annual NAACP Freedom Fund dinner, and William T. Patrick, former Detroit councilman, became visible participants in Federation activities.

This shift in the commitments of leadership coincided with a perceptible change in the tone of Cleage's public pronouncements. Shortly after the rebellion began, Cleage appeared as a weekly columnist in the *Michigan Chronicle*, which previously had seldom acknowledged his existence. For the first several months readers were treated to a strident, often bombastic, antiwhite militancy, in which Cleage threw every imaginable epithet at "the Man" and the system. As the internal struggle for leadership within the Negro community became more sharply defined, however, Cleage turned to a more positive posture. The militancy was still there, but his "Message to the Black Nation," as his column was entitled, contained less talk of "getting ready for guerilla warfare" and "preparing to die in the streets." Cleage began, instead, to emphasize unity in the black community, concentrating on themes of self-help and self-determination. Many observers took this apparent change in attitude as a decided improvement. Others interpreted it as indicative of Cleage's brilliance as a leader, a sign of his keen sense of timing and ability to judge the right moment to shift gears from a negative, antiestablishment rhetoric, to a more positive emphasis upon cohesiveness and solidarity within the Negro community. Whatever the true reasons were, it breathed new life into what initially appeared to be an abortive effort to achieve unity among Detroit's top Negro leadership. Ironically, however, it was this success which ultimately proved to be Cleage's undoing. By the spring of 1968 internal rumblings surfaced into an open breach between Cleage and younger militant members, resulting in the disbanding of the Federation for Self-Determination.

The Inner City Business Improvement Forum

While Cleage continued to enjoy his leadership role in the white press, his stock had once again tumbled in the black community, attendance at his church, now renamed the Shrine of the Black Madonna, declined drastically, and new focuses of power, such as the Inner City Business Improvement Forum, began to emerge.

In one sense, the rise and fall of Albert Cleage was inevitable, at least on the local level. The role of a black leader in today's society is at best precarious, and at worst impossible. It is questionable whether any one person can hope to incorporate under one banner all the perspectives on the racial problem that currently reside in the black community.

This difficulty was particularly acute for Cleage. He had the task not only of wooing the non-violent leadership forces to his cause, but also of continuing to give charismatic leadership to the diverse strands of black nationalism, some of which are separatists holding out for a geographic area within the United States where black people could migrate and establish their own nationhood, others of which are dedicated nihilists who see nothing beyond the necessity and inevitability of open racial warfare in the cities of America. Still others hold to the viewpoint that the cities of America are "the black man's land," to use the language of James and Grace Boggs, the philosophers of black nationalism in Detroit, and that ultimately they must and will be controlled by black people. This is Cleage's own personal philosophy, one with which a large number of Negroes agree, either conceptually or pragmatically. As to which philosophy, if any, will prevail remains an open question.

"The Monkey is Now on Cleage's Back"

Finally there are those who take the position that regardless of the ideological stances of the various strands of Negro leadership, even if some form of unity is achieved, it remains to be seen whether this unity can be extended to the Negro masses. Those with this view insist that no matter what conceptual posture Cleage or anyone else takes in the black community, ultimately the victory will go to whoever delivers—and delivery is defined in the time-honored traditional goals of the mass of Negro people: decent homes, good stable jobs, quality education, and fair and equitable law enforcement. Those who view the struggle in Detroit from this perspective argue that the large grants of money and influence to Cleage's organizations had a high risk attached to them, a risk that ultimately may have proved fatal to his leadership. As one of his fellow clerics observed several weeks after the riot, "The monkey is now on Cleage's back; he has to come through and deliver what the Negro masses want or else he will be in the same dilemma as the moderates."

Black Ministers

Two observations emerge out of the struggle for power as it is taking place in Detroit that have far-reaching significance. The first pertains to the vocations of the two dominant figures in the struggle—both are Negro clergymen. It should be of considerable interest to students of American Negro history that many of the key figures in the racial struggle have been black ministers. Nat Turner, leader of the famed Virginia slave revolt in the 1830s, was a Baptist cleric. Following his effort, slave states instituted a number of repressive measures against black slave religious movements. In some instances it became illegal to teach slaves to read, especially the Bible, and unlawful for slaves to assemble for worship unless a white person was present. In the present century the slain civil rights leader and Nobel Peace Prize winner Martin Luther King Jr. also was a Baptist pastor; James Farmer, longtime leader of the Congress on Racial Equality, is a graduate of Howard University's School of Religion; and Channing Phillips, the first black man to be nominated for President of the United States, is a militant Washington, D.C., clergyman. Even the Black Muslims, with their pronounced anti-white anti Christian philosophy, interpret the goals and aspirations of black people with a religious context.

Similarly, on the local level Albert Cleage, for all his black nationalist fervor, is nevertheless an Oberlin Seminary graduate and a clergyman in good standing in the United Church of Christ, although there are periodic rumors of attempts to oust him. Likewise, Roy A. Allen enjoys a position of prominence within Baptist circles in Detroit and serves on several municipal commissions and boards. To the extent that the racial struggle in America still finds its roots partially in religion, and that religious loyalties run deep in the mass of black people in America, some see a sign of hope. The religious temperament may prove to be a corrective to the spirit of despair and nihilism that grips growing numbers of young black people in America.

As the Cities Go, So Goes America

The second observation, however, is not so hopeful. Keen observers argue that even apart from the racial problems of big cities in America, urban society is so fraught with massive, critical dilemmas that its future is by no means certain. And black power—black control of the cities—is irrelevant to this future. Whether white men or black men make the decisions and determine political appointments and structure the economy is peripheral; it is like arguing who will be on the bridge or at the helm when the ship sinks. This analysis has within it the seeds of cynicism and despair, but at least one thing must be said for it. It recognizes that big cities in America are the most physically, socially, and economically vulnerable structures in contemporary society. And as the cities of America go, so goes the entire nation.

7. Riot Patterns

Was the Riot Organized or Spontaneous?

Many Americans find it difficult to believe that the riots of the past few summers have not been part of an organized conspiracy. Who the conspirators are, why they should plan and implement such large-scale disorders, and what they hope to achieve by them remains a matter of fierce debate. Nevertheless, a large segment of the American populace either suspects, is tentatively convinced, or firmly believes that none of the riots could have achieved such intensity or accomplished so much destruction without careful prior planning, and subsequent expert direction once they erupted.

However, an impressive number of citizens also rejects completely the conspiracy theory. They observe little if anything that occurred during the recent riots that cannot be explained as the cumulative result of centuries of racism in American society. This factor alone, they argue, complicated by the Viet Nam War, compounded by the existence of widespread poverty in an affluent society, and concentrated in the urban ghettos of our nation, is more than sufficient not only to trigger an explosion, but also to provide ample fuel for a prolonged conflagration.

As with any complex event, there may well be elements of truth in both interpretations. Taking either one seriously, however, has been made difficult by the refusal of each interpretation to allow for any truth in the other position. The conspiracy theory has become the province of the John Birch Society, which expends large sums of money holding seminars all across the United States, purporting to give the real facts behind the riots. Its members are convinced that there is a conspiracy and that the Communists are the principal conspirators. The Birch mentality has simultaneously refused to acknowledge that there could be anything wrong with American society that the eradication of twenty-two million Negroes and nine United States Supreme Court justices would not cure.

The ghetto theorists, on the other hand, deny the Communist-conspiracy approach. In their vehemence to lay this riot ghost to rest, they tend to disallow the possibility of any organized effort behind the riot. In one sense their position is more understandable, since they are legitimately concerned that the attention of the American public not be diverted from the sinkholes of American culture which are urban slums. But consciously or otherwise, the ghetto theorists are locked into an interpretation of the riots which is partially, if not primarily dictated by the answers they propose to urban violence. The solution to riots for this group is an expansion of the time-honored American answer for all its ills: spend more money. If the riots are more than just a cry of despair from the slums of America, then the ghetto theorists fear they have lost the major argument for massive efforts to eradicate the problems out of which riots are spawned.

What happened in Detroit in July 1967 is both comforting and confusing to both positions. The solution to the Detroit event and any other similar occurrence, however, will not be found until the facts supporting both viewpoints are put into perspective.

Police Intelligence Efforts

Those who doubt there was initial organization or planning behind the riot argue that police intelligence operations should have had some indication of impending trouble, and that in Detroit such intelligence was totally lacking. As a matter of fact, the police department and the mayor's summer task force spent major portions of the months of June and July tracing down rumors that trouble was planned for Detroit. On July 18, five days before the disorder actually occurred, the police special invesitgation bureau circulated a memorandum to top police executives detailing information received from three different sources on rumors of possible violence. The information was noteworthy to the extent that it correlated with earlier intelligence reports, all of which pointed to the first or second week in August as the target date. From a law-enforcement perspective, investigating a rumor is more difficult than a homicide investigation without a corpse; nevertheless, the memorandum carried a special notation to Superintendent Reuter that read, "The above rumors will receive this Bureau's continued attention and investigation."

Five days later the rumors had become fact. Whether there was substance to their description of what would happen and where, the police intelligence units never had time to ascertain. They were far too involved investigating the startling intelligence that began to flow in shortly after the disorder broke on Sunday morning.

The first report appears in the police disorder log at 10:20 a.m., Sunday, July 23. The special investigation bureau received an anonymous call from a woman alleging that she had been given information by a member of her family. According to the caller, "the persons who started the incidents on 12th street would do the same on Linwood and work downtown tonight." At noon an unidentified caller reported that the rioters would "assemble at Linwood and Joy, go to Grand River and then back to Woodward [precincts 10, 13] to help keep the riot going. Gangs [would] move from 12th street to Kercheval and back and forth" (precincts 13, 5). At 1:20 p.m. a white male reported to the desk sergeant at precinct 2 that while attempting to make a phone call from a public booth at the intersection of Grand River and Euclid, he was warned by an unidentified woman to get out of the area because there would be trouble (precinct 6 or 10). Then at 3 p.m. the mayor's task force reported information from a staff person in the city's poverty agency that the target date was to have been August 1, that four areas would be hit—12th street (precinct 10), Harper and Gratiot (precinct 15; areas three and four were unknown)—and that there were "25 paid snipers on the payroll." Finally, shortly before noon Sunday an officer on 12th street relayed to headquarters information received from bystanders that Grand River had already been or was about to be hit (precinct 6).

The significance of these reports lies in the time they were received and the pattern of the riot they projected. A confirmed report of rioting on Linwood, three blocks west of 12th street (precinct 10), was not received at headquarters until 3:25 p.m.; the first log entry of trouble on Grand River (precinct 6) appears at 4 p.m. Thus the intelligence anticipated by some four to five hours the actual movement of this disorder. Significantly also, the log notes confirmed reports of looting in downtown Detroit at 6:06 p.m., along Woodward avenue at 8:58 p.m. (precinct 13), and a "large fight" at Harper and Gratiot at 9:16 p.m. (precinct 15). The Harper-Gratiot intersection is the first entry pinpointing trouble on the city's far east side, and is the same location identified in the intelligence report received at 3 p.m., some six hours earlier!

In the pre-dawn hours of Monday morning the police communications center received a call from a citizen who identified himself and stated he had information relating to plans for the continuation of the disorder, and methods to be used for its escalation. He insisted on speaking to Girardin's assistant or "someone of equal authority," and was interviewed at 7:15 a.m. He lived in the riot area, was a member of the local selective service board, and related that he had been monitoring conversations on a citizen band radio giving orders on locations to be set afire. He claimed he heard orders to move the rioting to the east side of Detroit at least two hours before the public radio reports that trouble had erupted there.

Looting and Sniping

As the confusion of the first hours of the riot began to subside, the police were able to put together a vast amount of eye-witness reports concerning the pattern of the riot itself as it took place—first on 12th street and then throughout the city. Again and again witnesses reported that young men would appear on the scene in a commercial area, break store windows, and urge bystanders to help themselves. Those who broke windows or broke through doors were reported as not engaging in any looting; they seemed intent only on providing easy access and urging the crowds to loot. The looters in turn were described as consisting of two groups. In the first some men but mainly women took meat, apparel, and small appliances, and children took trinkets, cookies, or similar inexpensive items. At the same time, however, other looters apparently knew what they were doing and what they were after. According to witnesses, these persons wore leather gloves and heavy shoes, and some drove panel trucks or small vans. They are reported also to have concentrated on expensive and easily disposed of items: liquor, portable TVs and phonographs, and furs. Finally, a third group, distinct from the looters but possibly comprising those involved in the initial break-ins, were said to have returned and put looted stores to the torch.

One also has to take into account the peculiar patterns of gun-sniping that occurred approximately between 10 p.m. and midnight on the second, third, and fourth days of the riot. At about 11 p.m. on Monday, July 24, the scene of battle suddenly shifted from the streets to police and fire stations. Within a 50-minute period, nine different police and fire posts in widely separate parts of the city were under heavy sniper fire. Some of the officers present during this occurrence described it as being "under siege." The following night at about 10 the same drama began to unfold again; within a period of 70 minutes five police or fire locations were under sniper attack. On Wednesday the time pattern changed. After an 11-hour span, in which only nine unconfirmed reports of sniping were logged, gun fire suddenly erupted shortly before 3 p.m. An hour later two police or fire posts were under attack, and suspected snipers were observed in two other locations facing fire halls or police command posts. Soon after 10:30 p.m. gun fire opened up on two fire stations. (See Chapter 1 for a detailed account of these occurrences.)

Of considerable interest in each of these reports are the facts that the sniping activities were widely scattered throughout the city, occurred within a remarkably concentrated span of time, and ended with almost the same suddenness they began with. When combined with reports of a communications system allegedly used by the rioters, these observations constitute a major argument for the organization theory.

The organization theory becomes faulty, however, when it moves from the question of whether there was prior planning to who was involved. The eagerness of many to place blame for flaws in American society on external forces blinds them to developments and claims within our own nation, which at least ought to be taken at face value. Whatever else one might wish to say about the rise of black revolutionaries in America, it is this segment of the black community which has most clearly and unhesitatingly called for armed rebellion in America's urban ghettos and a strategy of violence which parallels to a remarkable degree the patterns of the summer riots of 1966 and 1967. This statement is only an observation, not an indictment, but it suggests that if the black revolutionaries lay claim openly to violence as a technique, perhaps they, rather than the Communists, ought to be taken seriously.

Detroit's Black Revolutionaries

The question of who Detroit's black revolutionaries are remains somewhat shrouded in mystery, in spite of local and national attempts to expose them. It seems axiomatic to many that the vocal and visible leaders of the post-riot rebellion are not

13. A fire-gutted "Beauty Salon" on 12th street.

14. Another fire-gutted building along 12th street.

15. A demolished "Pharmacy" on 12th street.

16. Detroit, July 1967.

the same persons as those who allegedly sparked the riot or those who fanned it into an experience in black urban revolution. The extent of contact or communication between these components, whether they share the same ideology or similar strategies, is debatable. What is clear is that Detroit has a small cadre of black revolutionaries committed to the proposition that American society, "the system," is pathologically corrupt, incapable of reform, and doomed to destruction. The black revolutionaries are as dedicated to bringing about that destruction as medical researchers are to eradicating cancer.

Factually, little is known about the black revolutionaries in Detroit or, for that matter, anywhere else. If, as some believe, they are analogous to underground-resistance movements during World War II or to terrorist groups in the Middle East, then it is not surprising that their structure, leadership, and personnel are not known. Nevertheless, black revolutionaries stand apart and are quite distinguishable from the mass of rioters on the one hand, and spokesmen for the post-riot rebellion on the other.

It is clear also that the black revolutionaries feel themselves to be part of an international struggle and identify the racial upheavals in America with those of emerging new nations in Africa, the political coups in Latin America, and the efforts toward self-determination in other parts of the world. That some contact is maintained between black revolutionaries in Detroit and other American cities seems apparent; it is, in fact, one of the frequent assertions of the revolutionaries themselves. Whether this contact extends to revolutionaries in other nations is uncertain; that they often quote a common body of revolutionary literature may indicate only a common ideology rather than actual communication.

In spite of pronouncements to the contrary, what the revolutionaries want is also ambiguous. The leaders of the post-riot rebellion have articulated two separate goals. One group, led by Cleage, argues for a "nation within a nation" concept, which essentially calls for black political and economic control of American cities. A second sphere of thought among nationalists extends this concept to argue for separate states where economic and political nationhood for black people can be achieved. The difference is basically one of geography rather than ideology. Whether the revolutionaries stand between or outside these two positions is unclear. Their ideological position seems to be that of total nihilism; they foresee the inevitability of open racial warfare in America and are determined to die as men fighting for selfhood rather than live as black slaves in an oppressive white world. That which seems to separate the revolutionaries from the rest of black nationalism is not simply their conceptual commitment to violence as a strategy, but their willingness to participate in the American experiences of urban violence. Whether the post-riot leaders of the rebellion in Detroit gave verbal support to a riot in which they had little if any actual participation remains questionable; that dedicated revolutionaries were involved in gun-sniping and arson incidents during the Detroit riot to many seems certain.

The Black Ghettos and Self-Determination

If the ghetto theorists were able to actually and accurately grasp the significance of black revolutionary thought and action, their perception of the racial struggle in America and its consequences would be greatly strengthened. In the final analysis, the slums of American cities are the pivotal factor in determining the future of urban culture in the United States and the fate of America's 22 million blacks, including those who have physically but not psychologically escaped ghetto boundaries. To focus, therefore, as the ghetto theorists do, on the plight of the American urban slum—the dilapidated housing, profiteering merchants, and absentee landlords, the disease, unemployment, and poverty—is not only important, it is even crucial to the outcome of the struggle. If an affluent, highly educated nation, which has the technological proficiency to achieve manned space flights and a sense of manifest destiny sufficient to permit it to involve enormous quantities of its resources and manpower in the affairs of nations on the other side of the globe, cannot or will not eradicate the poverty and slums in its midst, then it not only will have no future, it does not deserve one. At this point white liberals, Negro moderates, and black nationalists all share a common grievance: American ideals and the reality of American life are totally incompatible, and unless they are brought together, the future of this nation is in grave doubt.

At the same time the ghetto theorists fail to perceive the fundamental difference between American slums and ghettos. This error in perception has led to angry outbursts that decry the slums, but also to naive attempts to romanticize urban ghettos, to picture them as sub-cultures whose primary problem is one of a hostile white society. Social scientists, urbanologists, and writers have contributed enormously to this distorted view of ghetto life, and the distortion needs desperately to be clarified.

As many black people in the slums of our cities know all too well, there are evils in slum areas which go beyond profiteering merchants, lack of jobs, and absentee landlords. Crime figures in Detroit, for example, show that from 48 to 80 percent of the victims of homicides, rapes, street robberies, assaults, and burglaries are Negroes, most of whom live in the inner-city. Black recipients of city and state welfare programs know that they confront in these operations not only bureaucratic restrictions and regulations, but also the insensitivity and condescending paternalism of agency staff people, many of whom are also black. The children of slum inhabitants are also at the mercy of black narcotics pushers and black pimps, for whom the racial struggle, whether seen as a move toward integration or self-determination, means nothing. And black people in the slums also know that the merchants who over-charge for inferior goods and the landlords who exact high rents for slum residences are not all white.

Herein lies the dilemma of white liberalism and black nationalism. It is a problem that the massive amounts of money needed to physically eradicate slums can help resolve but not permanently cure. Ironically, in the final analysis it may be the strategy of black nationalist leaders like Albert Cleage, and the apparent successes of movements like the Black Muslims in changing the attitudes and aspirations of many black people from asocial to socially constructive behavior, which hold the key to solving this problem. In his 1968 New Year's message, Cleage proclaimed:

> Through the concept of self-determination, black militants have been able to give unity to a people fragmented by oppression and have begun the laborious process of transforming the black ghetto into a black community. Everywhere there is a growing black consciousness, black pride, black unity, and a growing commitment to black power. The building of this new self-image constitutes our accomplishment in 1967. During 1968 black militant leadership must so structure and program this new commitment to black power that it constitutes more than a willingness to die in the streets. The success of black militants in this basic task will determine the course of the Black Revolution for the next decade.

8. The Vulnerability of Our Cities

"A City with a Heart"

One of the lingering effects of a riot is that it forces those who live through it to look at the city from an entirely different perspective. In Detroit, perhaps, this is the one clear observation that can be made about the city as it emerged from its week of terror and destruction. Those who were involved in pre-riot Detroit and participated in the dynamics of its growth during the preceding five years saw the city in all of its creative potential —a city well along the road to economic recovery, with the tremendous educational, cultural, and spiritual resources that were to be found in its colleges and universities, its public schools, art and historical museums, churches and synagogues. It was a city that cared about its inhabitants—"a city with a heart," as the legend went—that had gained a national reputation for its pioneering efforts in the war against poverty, in fair and equitable law enforcement, in urban renewal, and in countless other critical areas of urban life. It was a city whose compassion was symbolized by the Torch Drive campaign, another pioneering Detroit effort, in which the city and its suburbs annually contributed over $25,000,000 to the financing of a vast network of private social service programs.

Needed: a New Dike

In the riot aftermath, however, one began to see the same urban landscape from a different vantage point. Problems that had always been visible, but had been blurred by the vision of progress, now emerged in sharper focus—the derelicts in the city's downtown parks and streets, the pimps prowling the streets in their Cadillacs, their girls lurking in doorways, the johns on their way home from downtown office buildings trying to make quick contacts in the central city before retreating to suburbia and respectability, the youths holding down street corners, the young mother on the bus with the look of indifferent despair, with six or eight or nine children in tow, on her way to some agency where she is a case number or a file card, and where she will sit for hours, waiting to tell her story to some public servant who will determine how well it does or does not fit a set of regulations concocted by people who consider such mothers and their broods a drain on the public economy. These are the cracks in the dike that holds back social chaos. It is little wonder that some have begun to believe that perhaps what we need is a new dike.

This post-riot perspective on the city is further sharpened by the recognition that in the minds of a majority of the city's inhabitants, who are white, decades if not generations of work by 90 percent of the Negro citizens of the city, who are taxpaying, law-abiding and community-conscious, and who because of their race, have been forced to make an extra contribution to community progress, are suddenly eclipsed by the events of one week in which, by the most generous calculation, less than 2 percent of the Negro citizens of the city participated. It suggests to many and convinces others of the futility of any attempt to build an authentic integrated community, and is grist for the mill of those who claim that at best separation, and at worst open racial conflict will be the ultimate solution to the racial problem in America.

"The System" in Shambles

Within this latter group there is that small but extremely articulate minority for whom racial warfare is not only a theoretical possibility but also an imminent reality, and they are prepared to make the most of it. The extent of this group's participation in the Detroit riot is not known; in fact, the exact or even approximate number of people who cherish this conviction is not known either. What is known is that this group, for decidedly different reasons, includes both Negroes and whites, and that their number grows as each successive wave of urban violence sweeps across this nation. For both racial components in this group there is the deeply held conviction, again for drastically different reasons, that American society, "the system," is in shambles, that the cities of America are tragically symbolic of this societal confusion, and that in some form or other violence is inevitable. Black advocates of this viewpoint will dwell on the historic injustices of American society—the discrimination against, and the oppression and exploitation of America's black minority—problems that are horrendous when they emerge in the context of urban culture. Their white counterparts—and ironically both black and white people who share this philosophy of America's plight share also a strangely identical perspective in psychology and strategy—are convinced that it is the hordes of blacks in our cities who create the most pressing problems of urban culture: crime, slums, illegitimacy, and welfare costs. In the minds of these persons the restless and ruthless blacks, aided unwittingly by a left-wing U.S. Supreme Court and deceptively by the Communists, will ultimately bring this nation to ruin unless they are stopped.

What makes both of these perspectives so appalling is the awful extent to which our cities are physically, socially and psychologically vulnerable to assaults from either side, once either group moves from theory to action. The physical vulnerability of our cities is difficult to assess without creating widespread panic and hysteria. And yet we court physical disaster if we do not candidly and realistically face this problem.

135

Much of the post-riot debate about police action in the early stages of the Detroit riot was inappropriate, if not irrelevant, because it failed to consider this possibility. The question, therefore, should not have been whether the Detroit police responded adequately to the events of Sunday, July 23. Given the nature of the Detroit civil disorder, and of those that preceded it in Watts, Hough and Newark-Plainfield, the question should have been whether any response by a local law enforcement agency, working at maximum strength and under optimum conditions, is adequate to quell the emerging, new patterns of civil disorders without wide-spread destruction, loss of life, and pathological damage to the city's internal structure. The emphasis here is on pathological damage, since there is little doubt that in some cities in America, damage to their habits, attitudes, policies and prejudices is not only in order, but long overdue. The issue remains, however, as to whether this can be done by a strategy of violence, and whether the local law enforcement agency can effectively cope with that violence.

It is the latter part of this issue that is critically related to the problem of vulnerability. There are certain strategic locations in any city whose functioning is indispensable to the life of that city—water pumping stations, public or private power plants, buildings that house the intricate network of communications systems, fire stations and equipment. Any disruption in the orderly functions of these systems is disaster for a city. There are also less vital but equally vulnerable aspects of any modern, urban, industrial area—freeway bridges and overpasses, chemical plants, large storage facilities for explosive liquids and gases. Sabotaging any of these installations would create unimaginable panic and chaos in the city.

The physical structure of the city also lends itself to havoc when it becomes, for example, a sniper's nest. The rooftops of a group of two-story commercial structures on a busy thoroughfare can be a most effective base of operation for a sniper skilled in the hit-and-run technique. One man, working from such a vantage point, can pin down or tie up several squads of police and firemen, and then be off to another spot before his location can be pinpointed and the buildings surrounded. Finally, a dozen persons with the necessary equipment and sufficient pre-planning can set enough fires to turn a city into a raging inferno.

It was the potential of any one, or a combination of these possibilities developing, that necessitated the Detroit police response not only to the riot area itself, but also the deployment of police personnel to guard all vital installations in the city. These posts had to be held until enough guardsmen arrived to provide relief. In sheer numbers it is impossible for a local police agency to deploy sufficient manpower to cope effectively with a disturbance that included between 300 to 500 people when the first alert was given and thousands within a few hours, to simultaneously provide security for all the city's vital installations, to continue responding to urgent requests for police service—automobile accidents involving injuries, hold-up alarms, suicide attempts, critically ill children—and finally to maintain sufficient personnel in the rest of the city to control any situation, criminal or otherwise, that might develop, either spontaneous or planned.

The Federal Government and the Cities

For these reasons the post-riot response of the President of the United States to the Detroit disaster, contained in a September 14, 1967, speech to the International Association of Chiefs of Police convention in Kansas City, was remarkable in its shortsightedness. Ignoring the ill-chosen language used to characterize the officials who were involved in the riot, the burden of his remarks was to reiterate the time-honored American myth that law enforcement is a local responsibility. Not only was this posture ironic for a political leader who has not been renowned for any hesitancy to impose federal intervention in all sorts of situations, from Viet Nam to proposed copper price hikes, it was incredibly unrealistic. As well informed as the White House was kept during the entire riot, if the facts of what happened in Detroit are known anywhere, they should have been known and understood there.

If in fact the Detroit experiences of July 1967 are ever repeated, then the issue will not be whether there will be federal intervention or assistance, but when. Assuming that the strength of the state police is inadequate for this task (in some states state troopers are prevented by law from being used in riots or smaller civil disorders) and that they will also be a necessary line of defense for smaller cities to which the riot fever might spread, as it did in Michigan,* and assuming also that the strength and capability of the National Guard also are inadequate, the major urban centers of our nation have no alternative except to have the prompt assistance of federal troops. The existence of a specially trained cadre of such troops, containing a high complement of Negro officers and strategically deployed at several military bases around the nation, which could have been mobilized, airlifted, and committed to action in Detroit at the same time that police officers were called up, would have put federal troops on the street by noon on Sunday, instead of 2 a.m., Tuesday. That might have made a difference!

Urban Decay or Urban World Culture?

The vulnerability of our major cities has to do not only with their physical openness to assault, at a deeper level it is the problem of the vulnerability of urban culture itself. In 1956 Dr. H. Warren Dunham, a distinguished social scientist, was elected by his colleagues at Wayne State University to be Leo M. Franklin Memorial Professor in Human Relations for that year. His final lecture in a series of six on "The City in Mid-Century" was appropriately entitled "Prospects for Human Relations in the Urban Environment." Professor Dunham's comments in his Introduction to the printed volume have proven to be prophetic in the light of events of the past few summers. He wrote:

---

*Two days after the Detroit riot began, smaller outbreaks occurred in six other Michigan cities.

138

The city as it exists in our time is faced with two possible outcomes. The one, it may contain such deeply imbedded elements of decay or prove to be so at the mercy of the new forms of energy that it will decline in power and influence, thus giving way to new forms of community organization. If this happens, our time will be recorded in history as a finale to the age of great cities. The other, the city may continue into an indefinite future if we demonstrate that we can secure a more conscious control over the processes that determine and shape its development. If this happens, our time will be recognized as the period when man took a great evolutionary forward stride by being able to obtain a sufficient control over the growth pattern of his cities to lay the foundation for an urban world culture. To grasp clearly the implications of these two possible outcomes, it becomes essential to understand the factors responsible for urban growth and decay. (*The City in Mid-Century*, Detroit 1956, p. 3.)

To say that we have not made significant progress on either front is to state the obvious. A number of reasons for this lack of progress are apparent. One factor has been the rapidity of the growth of the urban complex itself; American cities have expanded at such a pace that it has been difficult to effectively observe, not to mention to adequately judge the substance or direction of urban life. Another factor has been the degree to which social scientists, to whom we look for insight and understanding of man in his social, political, religious and cultural environment, have been limited if not thrown completely off course by their traditional assumptions that the growth and development of cities is analogous to that of the human organism, with a built-in mechanism which, in Dunham's words, "permitted it an internal healing of its ills as it moved through time" (*City in Mid-Century*, p. 156). A third factor has undoubtedly been the tragic gap between what insights the social scientists have been able to muster about the urban environment, and the policies and practices of the decision-makers—city administrators, politicians and industrialists, city planners and municipal board members—

whose judgments actually determine issues of public housing, urban renewal, parks and freeways, schools and sewage disposal plants, the quality of law enforcement, and a host of similar problems.

If the observation that we have not made progress on these fronts is obvious, then the riots become a symbolic way of expressing the sense of urgency that is involved. Post-riot Detroit, for example, faces the practical necessity of rebuilding the rather sizable commercial and residential areas destroyed during the week of July 23. It faces in this task a dilemma, in the classic Greek sense of the word! On the one hand, if the city returns to business as usual, and rebuilds the same problems back into the devastated areas—small pawnshops and loan agencies, bars and taverns, poolrooms and fourth-rate furniture stores—it builds the ingredients for another explosion. And yet, if it rebuilds with a conscious effort to eliminate the problems of slums, overcrowding and exploitation, it unwittingly gives credence to the theory that violence is a way to achieve social change; the riot thereby becomes an exercise in instant urban renewal.

Assuming, however, that even dilemmas are resolvable and that American cities are not the first in history to have experienced destructive civil disorders, the challenge becomes one of minimizing the vulnerability of our urban centers, both physically and culturally. The city of Paris, for example, was laid out after the French Revolution to more effectively achieve riot control; such physical redesigning of American cities may or may not be ethical, feasible or practical, but it does raise the possibility of reassessing such modern urban practices as the apparently unlimited expansion of freeways, developments that present headaches to law enforcement agencies, destroy enormous tracts of taxable property, erode the critical supply of central city housing, and primarily benefit suburban residents who want the best of both worlds—both the economic and cultural advantages of the city proper, and the escape from its most critical problems which the bedroom communities of America offer. It certainly calls into grave question the wisdom of such developments as those seen by renowned city planner Constantine Doxiadis, who describes the urban environment as moving rapidly toward a time when Detroit, for example, will be the hub of a megalopolis, a continuous ribbon of urban-suburban complexes running from Chicago on the west to Cleveland on the east.

The American Compulsion to Flee the City

The primary challenge, however, remains that of creating a new style of life in urban culture, one that not only eliminates the ingredients that spawn riots, but also deals creatively with a myriad of urban problems—crime, anomie, the breakdown of family life, poverty, and rootlessness. In this regard we may have much to learn from the insights of anthropologist Edward T. Hall, a pioneer in the field of intersocietal communications and one of a small group of social scientists seeking ways to make our cities fit for human habitation. Hall's work, as reported in the Autumn 1967 issue of *Horizon*, deals with the need of humans to have a certain amount of space in which to conduct their daily lives. Unless we study this need, he maintains, and the extent to which it varies among people of different ethnic and cultural backgrounds, life in our cities, where ethnic-cultural diversity is greatest, can become intolerable. The plight of our cities has risen primarily because the American people have never taken the city seriously except as a matter of economic convenience. There is a nostalgia in the American mentality which still dreams of the cozy cottage, set in the midst of an expansive, rolling lawn, preferably near a lake, and located in a small village or town, as the ideal life-style. Symbolic of today's American city are its freeways in the early morning and late afternoon rush hours, with thousands of people flocking into the city in the morning to partake of its promises and rushing out in the evening to escape its responsibilities. Unless we change this pattern and perspective—and soon—American cities may prove to have been the arena for the final death throes of a national culture.

III
Epilogue

Epilogue

Detroit After the Riot

Whether Detroit, two years after the worst urban upheaval in 20th century America, has recovered or learned anything from its devastating experience remains an open question. Viewed from the perspective of the black community, many of the signs are hopeful. The rhetoric of the first few months has gradually been replaced by substantial efforts, created and led by black community leaders and financed in large measure by their white counterparts, to establish black-owned businesses and housing developments. Growing political solidarity is also evident, with new coalitions formed to challenge the traditional political machinery and alliances of the city. Post-riot studies continue to affirm a significant commitment on the part of the majority of Detroit's black populace to the goal of an integrated community, but this traditional goal is balanced by a more introspective concern with the development of a strong, viable black community, with an ability to enter into bi-racial dialogue from a position of strength rather than a posture of accommodation.

The city itself, however, remains a paradox. Viewed from this broader perspective, Detroit reflects a paralysis of nerve and

145

effort. Most of the liberal-progressive premises on which its social and economic programs had been based in the five years before the riot were called into grave question by that event, and no new premises or programs have emerged to take their place. The sweeping recommendations of the Mayor's Development Team for the reorganization of city government remain unimplemented, leadership from city hall seems increasingly ineffective, polarization between Detroit's black and white community continues to harden, and liberal elements in the city appear confused and uncertain in which direction to move. And while inertia grips political and civic leadership, the problems of crime continue to mount, businesses accelerate their flight from the central city to the suburbs, the schools face financial disaster, and rumors of tax increases abound. In 24 months the city of hope has become the city in crisis.

Nowhere in Detroit has this crisis emerged in sharper focus than in the tragic and volatile area of police-Negro relations. Detroit, until July 1967, was considered to be the city that had found a solution to this problem and was moving aggressively to implement it. In 1965 and 1966, 2,400 Detroit policemen, over half the total force, underwent an intensive, 20-hour course in race relations. It was the first such massive in-service training ever undertaken by any police department in the nation. Detroit's civilian-police precinct meetings, its citizens complaint bureau, and its youth service corps became models in police-community relations techniques throughout the nation. By determined effort the police department doubled the number of black officers on its force in 18 months, and while the total ratio of black to white policemen was still pitifully small, the city managed in this short time to reverse a recruitment process that had been entrenched for a century. Just a few weeks before the riot broke the department had enrolled the first class of student patrolmen that was 50 percent black.

But post-riot Detroit has been plagued by a continual escalation of hostilities between police officers and black citizens. Several inflammatory confrontations have only served to focus added tension to almost daily complaints from the black com-

munity that police officers refuse service to Negro neighborhoods, and there is an equal volume of complaints from officers
that their very presence in black sections of the city is met with
anger, suspicion, and aggressiveness. In this tense atmosphere
the Algiers Motel incident, which occurred on the third night
of the riot and in which three Detroit police officers were indicted
for the murder of two black youths, has emerged in black minds
as the prototype of police-black conflict, of racist police officers
arrayed against helpless black victims. In an ironic sense, however, the Algiers Motel incident may prove to portray much more
than this; it may well represent in microcosm the whole en-
tangled, complex problem of what is wrong with the police
system in urban America.

The Algiers Motel Incident in Retrospect

Of all the events that transpired in Detroit during the week of
July 23, 1967, the Algiers Motel incident stands out as the most
bizarre occurrence. Novelist John Hersey, who has discussed the
episode at length (*The Algiers Motel Incident*, New York 1968),
described it as containing "all the mythic themes of racial strife
in the United States: the arm of the law taking the law into its
own hands; interracial sex; the subtle poison of racist thinking by
'decent' men who deny that they are racists; the societal limbo
into which so many young black men have been driven . . . ambiguous justice in the courts; and the devastation in both black
and white human lives that follows in the wake of violence."
As real as these issues are, they mask the far deeper problem
of the nature and structure of the police system in American
cities, and the critical question, given this nature and structure,
of whether there is any hope for significant change or reform in
its operation. To this issue, what happened at the Algiers Motel
is tragically enlightening. While the incident itself was unique in
a horrendous sense, the policemen involved who were identified
and indicted for murder were not. They were young officers, with
from three to five years on the force, who had grown up in De-

147

troit, attending its schools, colleges, and churches, working in its YMCAs, and serving in its Boy Scout programs. In terms of their background, education, and experience, they were typical of today's young police officer in any large city in America.

Those who blame the police, either for recruiting such individuals in the first place or for failing to give them proper training after they were hired, condemn the wrong culprit. Police officers who are white are drawn from the same culture of prejudice and bigotry toward blacks—what the Kerner Commission Report calls "white racism"—as are white teachers, social workers, shop foremen, computer programmers, and members of any other occupation. Some police officers overcome this burden, others suppress it, still others never rid themselves of it. Unfortunately, however, no one to date has developed a psychological test for diagnosing white racism; consequently it is not discovered until, as in the Algiers Motel incident, it is too late. But to expect police training of any type to erase 21 years of white attitudes, white perspectives, and white stereotypes concerning blacks is to indulge in wishful thinking. The blame for such persons being in police uniforms should be placed not so much on the police department and its recruiting process as on the community that creates such individuals in the first place.

At the same time, and no matter where the blame belongs, police systems cannot tolerate racists in their ranks. Police work is fraught with far too many daily human conflict situations to be able to afford officers whose biases control their behavior. The problem, however, involves not only weeding out such officers, but also the recognition that because police systems are structured as they are, racist attitudes frequently become enhanced and entrenched by the very nature of the officer's daily routine. The police in any society are given the primary responsibility of dealing with criminal offenders; if this continual contact with robbers, rapists, muggers, and murderers takes place in the core sections of American cities where crime is high and residents are black, it is sufficient to warp the racial perspective of the best of men. And, if this perspective is limited or biased at the outset, bad matters are made worse.

The Algiers Motel incident also makes appallingly clear the extent to which the attitudes of police officers are warped by duty assignments involving the control of vice, especially prostitution, and by prolonged exposure to inner city precincts. If the interviews with the three policemen indicted for murder that Hersey recounts in his book are accurate, and there is no reason to doubt that they are, they reveal two significant facts about the social perspective of many white police officers: an enormous antipathy toward black prostitutes, ironically balanced by an almost compassionate attitude toward their primarily white clientele, and an almost total lack of contact with black citizens other than in their capacities as police officers.

The latter problem is beyond the ability of any police department to regulate, but the former—vice duty—is not. Controlling prostitution consumes almost as much police personnel time and energy as controlling traffic. Both tasks have become highly developed police specialties, both lend themselves to bribery and corruption, and both are dramatic examples of what has gone wrong with the police system in urban America.

In dealing with the problems of traffic and prostitution, both control and enforcement are vested in the same person, the policeman. In traffic enforcement he can ticket delivery trucks which double park or block alleys, or overlook them if the store owner remembers him at Christmas time. In vice control he can arrest prostitutes in some bars or in certain areas, and look the other way in others. In an increasing number of traffic accidents the policeman functions as a tax-supported employee of insurance companies who refuse to settle for damages unless an elaborate, quasi-scientific police report has been compiled. Likewise in arresting prostitutes, policemen who work in clean-up squads or the "whore-car" have developed complicated devices for snaring the women involved. Ironically, less time and energy would be expended if police attention were directed to the purchasers of prostitute services. In this regard, at least one of the benefits of the July 1967 riot was its contribution to the decline of prostitution; white johns are much more cautious about prowling the streets of the central city than before.

Whether this cautiousness has a long-term effect remains to be seen. More important is the recent discovery by municipalities that the application of technology to problems of traffic control has far greater effectiveness than the continued use of a scarce supply of police officers. An equally important step can be taken when cities also recognize that police personnel are unnecessary for traffic enforcement. There is nothing that police officers do in traffic enforcement that could not be accomplished just as well by trained civilian personnel.

In similar fashion, and once American society frees itself of hypocritical views on the problem, the control of prostitution could be accomplished much more efficiently and effectively by non-police agencies. If there is concensus that the trade cannot be abolished, then there should also be the recognition that its control is much more a health problem, and its practitioners are cases more for psychologists, priests, and psychiatrists, than for policemen. European cities have found methods to deal with prostitution with greater realism and effectiveness, and without all the collateral criminal by-products that prostitution breeds in American cities.

Redefining the Police Function in Urban America

Currently in American society, however, handling traffic and prostitutes are only two of an unbelievable array of police functions and responsibilities that, when taken as a whole, make the task of today's policeman virtually impossible. He is expected to catch criminals, protect children at school crossings, stop riots, mediate family quarrels, deliver babies, control the sale of liquor, run a municipal ambulance service, recover missing mental patients, discipline rebellious youths, protect demonstrators in some instances and arrest them in others—the list is endless.

American society has somehow managed to lump these diversified services under the heading "law enforcement" and to invest their performance in men who are high school graduates but, according to statistics, drawn primarily from the bottom 25 percent of their class. These men are then inducted into a system operated on strict military principles and procedures; their most important virtue becomes the ability to take orders without question or comment and to apply the necessary force when situations warrant it. If they are assigned to traffic duty they function in the same fashion, giving orders the public must obey. But the same technique applied to street demonstrations or family disputes is apt to be totally ineffective, or even worse, to trigger reactions of hostility or aggressive outrage. Police conduct during the Columbia University rebellion and the Chicago Democratic Convention in the spring and fall of 1968 was atrocious beyond question, but the greater tragedy is that the police were forced to resolve conflict situations they had no part in creating in the first place, and to do so by relying on their quickest defense but the worst possible device for dealing with political confrontations —force.

To speak of resolving the dilemma of law enforcement by professionalizing its personnel without changing its internal structure is like trying to cure cancer with aspirin tablets. Professionalization, among other things, implies the creation of highly trained and skilled personnel who are able to think independently and make individual judgments based on examinations of rational alternatives in problem-solving situations. Such a process is in basic and unalterable conflict with a system that operates on military principles and involves the performance of a myriad of tasks, all of which no rational person would ever undertake.

Resolving this problem, therefore, will have to begin with a total reassessment of the nature and structure of law enforcement in urban society. The police function needs to be redefined in American cities in such a way that may well consign the traditional policeman's role to oblivion. In its place cities can create a number of civilian occupations, filled by persons trained to perform a number of the non-law enforcement functions policemen currently handle: family disputes, ambulance runs, the processing of all types of municipal and state licenses—from bicycles to the sale of liquor—traffic control and enforcement. Then a competently trained and highly skilled group of criminal investigators can be organized to deal exclusively with crime control and prevention, concentrating their energies on this enormously critical task.

Such a development might also enable police departments to develop greater proficiency in waging the battle against crime. Currently that battle is being lost, for even allowing for the paper increase in crime statistics (more crime is being reported and counted than in past years), police departments nevertheless are solving at best only about 25 percent of the crimes that are reported. And while the reasons for this inability of society in general to gain control over the rising crime rate are many and complex, a central and frequently unexamined aspect of the problem relates directly to the fact that most police systems are antiquated bureaucracies, using inadequate methods, outmoded weaponry, and overburdened personnel to grapple with one of the nation's most vexing problems.

Police systems today, in spite of their inherent weaknesses, do somehow manage to produce a number of dedicated, hard-working, honest and humane police officers. But the same systems spawn an appalling number of hard-bitten, cynical and indifferent "cops" who detest their work, take from it whatever they can get and by any means available, and bitterly resent the citizens they serve. From the latter ranks come not only the cases of police brutality but also the cases of bribery, scandal and corruption, which periodically plague every major police department in the United States.

Urban society in America will have to face the brutal fact that the reasons for such a situation lie as much with the society and its police system as they do with those men who disgrace it. A society which values property above persons, which is outraged by street crime but is indifferent to "white collar" and organized crime, which encourages the principle that everyone has his price, and which demands that police officers control the problems that the society creates, gets the kind of law enforcement it deserves. And that law enforcement, structured as it currently is, will continue to be mediocre no matter who runs the system or the color of the men who fill its ranks.

This last point is frequently lost on those who are convinced that by replacing white policemen with black recruits, the problem of police-community relations will be solved. Black police officers do bring to the task of law enforcement a greater awareness and sensitivity to the problems of black people—one would not expect it to be otherwise. But black policemen are no more immune than their white colleagues to the emotional stress of the system, the schizophrenic strain of the dual standards of American justice, or the temptations to be "on the take." And since it is the system itself that needs restructuring, rather than merely changing the color of its components, society ought to begin where the problem really is, and not simply continue to tinker with its abuses.

Restructuring the police system is one of the most critical and difficult tasks cities could conceivably undertake. But if the need is acknowledged and the possible benefits are recognized, the task itself might begin at two essential points. The first involves the recognition that form follows function, that the image of the police officer cannot be changed unless what he does and how he goes about it change first. Cities can begin by taking all municipal duties and services not directly related to crime control out of police departments and lodging them in other, more appropriate civilian-staffed agencies. Ambulance service and the control of prostitution should be responsibilities of health departments, with the latter a crime problem only to the extent that pandering and street or organized prostitution are involved. Traffic can be handled by departments of streets and traffic or merged into departments of transportation, where the vast and intricate problems that produce the urban snarl can be systematically studied, coordinated, controlled, and hopefully unravelled. The issuing and control of all licenses, including liquor, should be given to a bureau created for such purposes; efficiently run, it could represent new sources of revenue for city coffers. Monitoring family disputes may continue to be a police function, but mediating them need not be. Family service centers can create teams of trained personnel to respond to such crises, with backup services of policemen if weapons are involved, and to give continued professional assistance, which policemen cannot give.

By thus freeing the police system of from 40 to 60 percent of its current responsibilities, police departments can then concentrate their full energies and resources on crime itself, with more personnel available for street patrol and criminal investigation, and less varied assignment responsibilities in which to demand proficiency. Police personnel can then be trained for one principal function—crime control—and be provided with the best scientific insights and technological tools with which to accomplish this task.

In creating what is basically a new role for urban police officers, college training should be encouraged as an eligibility requirement for acceptance, if college-level studies are presumed to be of benefit in police-community relations, although in the Algiers Motel incident, ironically, two of the three officers indicted for murder would have met this requirement. College training certainly should be a prerequisite for promotion in the police system, on the assumption that it represents the best device society has created for developing leadership skills.

The creation of a new perspective on law enforcement itself is as essential as the redefinition and reassignment of traditional police duties. Police departments can and should be run in the same fashion as public utilities; they can be managed as effectively operated businesses instead of like military installations. Policemen can be made conscious of the service they perform for the public if the system of rewards places a premium upon excelling in this manner rather than as it currently operates—by simply rewarding longevity. Merit pay and promotions should be based upon a carefully balanced system which evaluates an officer's progress in furthering his education, his skill as a criminal investigator, and his public conduct; if he fails to measure up in any of these areas, he should be firmly encouraged to find employment elsewhere, rather than protected as an ineffective but permanent member of a fraternal guild.

These observations are neither new nor exhaustive. To the

extent that there is any merit in them, it is in the fact that they are commonplace in every other major institutional process, but have never been tried in law enforcement. Society does not need nor can it tolerate future Algiers Motel incidents. It almost guarantees them, however, if it does not drastically alter the burdens it imposes upon its policemen. Equally basic, if not of greater fundamental importance to the future of urban America, is enabling the police system to gain the ability to do its job effectively and to regain the public confidence as it goes about the task. Neither accomplishment is possible without the other, and if either fails, the battle to save America's cities is lost also.

Random Reflections: A Half-Century After

That Detroit survived one of the catastrophic episodes of civil disorder in the nation's history is one of the remarkable stories of urban America. No one at the time, however, realized that the riot's aftermath would be almost, in some respects, a greater calamity for the city than the riot itself. Only with the passage of time have we come to see the significance of larger issues and dilemmas that were buffeting Detroit's existence, that have affected its recovery and that continue to hang like a pall over many of the nation's urban communities.

Of those issues, none loomed larger nor of greater consequence than what we have subsequently come to recognize as the deindustrialization of urban America. Detroit has felt its impact more than any other major urban community; five decades after the riot, the decline and fall of Motown as the industrial hub of the nation is the occurrence that has left the city with its most visible, massive scars.

When the riot broke out, Detroiters who were trying to address issues of equal employment opportunity and the quality of the public schools, of discrimination in places of public accommodation (which, believe it or not was still an issue in Detroit in the 1960s) and of police-community relations (as it was euphemistically termed in that era) failed completely to see the tidal wave of deindustrialization that was approaching its precincts with relentless fury. Five decades later its scars still mar the city's landscape. The Packard plant, which opened in 1903 as an industrial landmark on East Grand Boulevard, closed in 1958. GM's Fisher Body plant closed in 1974. The Dodge Main plant, which, at its peak, employed 30,000 workers, closed in 1980. The Ford Rouge plant—the crown jewel of automobile manufacturing and symbol of the industrial era in America—went from 90,000 workers in 1930 to 30,000 workers in 1960 to 6,000 in 1990.

Between plant closures, the shift in manufacturing sites from cities in the north to less-labor friendly sites in the south, and the ruthless advance of automation, Detroit in the 1950s and 1960s was being savaged by forces beyond its control. In retrospect, its riot can be seen as a nightmare episode in a bad dream of industrial despair from which the city is just beginning to awake.

Slowly, Detroit is finding new forms of activity to revitalize its economic life. While neither of the size or scope that would begin to replace car manufacturing, these new enterprises offer the promise of job opportunities that reflect the demands of the digital age. As these economic efforts hopefully expand, they present the city with new challenges; as the poet James Russell Lowell would have it—"new occasions teach new duties; time makes ancient good uncouth." As Detroit makes its way back from the brink of urban collapse, it may well point the way for other cities whose problems and difficulties are much the same.

It is noteworthy that since World War I, major civil disorders have been cyclical in their occurrence in America. From the riots in Tulsa and St. Louis in 1918, to Detroit in 1943, to the more than fifty cities that exploded in the mid-sixties, to the Los Angeles riot in 1992, to the more recent series of clashes that have taken place in Baltimore, suburban St. Louis, and elsewhere, civil disorders appear almost generational in character. It is as if every quarter-century, unaddressed or unresolved conflicts are experienced by a new cohort of city dwellers who lack memory of earlier clashes and whose anger and outrage burst conventional bounds. It would be hoped that this might serve both as a warning and a spur to civic leaders to get their urban houses in order—to place a greater sense of urgency on tackling problems of inequality and injustice. Only time will tell.

In 1967, all eyes were focused on the Detroit police and their role, both in the events that led to the city's explosion and in restoring order to the devastated city. National pundits took note of the similar role of the police in every other city that erupted between 1964 and 1968. A half-century later, nothing has essentially changed. New theories of policing are tried, more training is given to patrol officers, but clashes between police and civilians continue to be the igniting incident in the nation's repeated wave of civil disorders. They also continue to be triggered by the most trivial of police-citizen encounters—a traffic stop for a defective taillight, selling untaxed cigarettes, jaywalking, expired license tags—and increasingly with fatal results. Many ask whether a better display of judgment on the part of the police might reduce such encounters. Others wonder if the time-worn management practice in policing of using the number of tickets written by an officer as a measure of diligence and alertness could not be replaced by more effective means of performance evaluation. Nearly everyone—police and citizens alike—hopes that some way will be found to heal the breach between the police and the people.

Now that the first decades of the digital age have left their mark, we have the opportunity and the obligation to assess what this new era means for American society and for cities like Detroit, which barely managed to survive the collapse of the industrial period. How do we especially avoid the danger that the benefits of the new era will be celebrated or taken for granted while the problems it creates will be minimized or ignored?

Detroit presents almost an entirely new physical setting in which to rebuild itself. In one bizarre sense, the riot was an exercise in instant urban renewal. Large swaths of the city's residential areas were abandoned in the riots' aftermath; these are the empty houses the media likes to display when it depicts contemporary Detroit. Rather than an eyesore, the vast tracts of uninhabited land present an unexcelled opportunity both to constrain the size of the city and to design and build a new urban community for the digital age. Detroit has lost almost one million residents since 1950, but they are slowly being replaced by younger, technologically astute workers, both Black and white, for whom the city's center is no longer the habitation of the poor and the dispossessed but instead an opportunity to enjoy good restaurants, entertainment centers, and other benefits of urban living.

The challenge, in large part, is how to continue to attract the new, younger urbanites and simultaneously find a place for those who were once the backbone of the workforce in the previous industrial period. This is not just Detroit's challenge; it is a problem of national scope ad significance. In Detroit's case, a service economy that takes advantage, for example, of health care–related employment opportunities in the city's world-renowned medical and medical research facilities might be able to create jobs for the unskilled, as well as for the newer generation of Detroiters.

The reawakening of this grand and proud old city is a testament to the resiliency of its residents who have refused to give up on their hometown but also to a tradition of coping with adversity that stretches over at least three centuries. In 1805, in the aftermath of a fire that leveled the city, Fr. Gabriel Richards penned what has become Detroit's motto: "It arises from ashes; we hope for better things."

That hope is well on its way to a new realization.

Hubert G. Locke, 2016

Index

Index

Unions, 117
United Automobile Workers, 17, 38, 63
United Community League For Civic Action, 26-27
United Community Services, 64, 65, 101-102
U.S. Department of Justice, 65
U.S. Supreme Court, 53, 124, 135
University of Chicago, 112
University of Detroit Law School, 68, 77
University of Michigan, 102
"Urban Challenge, The," 68
Urban League, 55, 117

Vance, Cyrus R., 20, 37-38, 42, 48, 85, 93, 102, 113
Viet Nam War, 74, 123, 137

Virginia Park Rehabilitation Council, 29-30

Walk to Freedom, 61
Washtenaw County Jail, 77
Watts, 136
Wayne County Jail, 77
—Prosecutor, 96
—Sheriff, 50-51, 77
Wayne State University, 54, 102, 104, 138
West Central Organization, 114
White, Horace A., 112
Williams, G. Mennen, 20, 56, 66, 88
Winkelman, Stanley, 104
Witherspoon, Julian, 29
Wolverine Bar Association, 119
World War II, 129
WXYZ, 100-101

YMCA, 54, 60, 148

CPSIA information can be obtained
at www.ICGtesting.com
Printed in the USA
BVOW06s1444140817
491738BV00009B/22/P